CW01304588

Living with God

by

Raven

AuthorHouse™ UK Ltd.
500 Avebury Boulevard
Central Milton Keynes, MK9 2BE
www.authorhouse.co.uk
Phone: 08001974150

© *2008 Raven. All rights reserved.*

No part of this book may be reproduced, stored in a retrieval system, or transmitted by any means without the written permission of the author.

First published by AuthorHouse 2/25/2008

ISBN: 978-1-4343-6048-9 (sc)

Printed in the United States of America
Bloomington, Indiana

This book is printed on acid-free paper.

Acknowledgements

Angels are on hand to help us on every step of our journey in this life. This book came into publication because two angels stepped forward when the time was right to bring the lessons within it to you.

Thank you, **Dr George Macleod and Mrs Dorothy Macleod**, your gift of publishing this book is far greater than you will ever know.

Contents

Chapter 1	Something had to give	1
Chapter 2	Emma	9
Chapter 3	The Good Doctor	14
Chapter 4	The out of body experience	21
Chapter 5	The reunion with Emma	28
Chapter 6	Leave everything and follow me	35
Chapter 7	Meeting the Angel	40
Chapter 8	Materialism	61
Chapter 9	Canada	65
Chapter 10	The end of one creation and the beginning of another	71
Chapter 11	Trust	110
Chapter 12	The Awakening	126
	The Awakening	128
Chapter 13	The Decree Absolute	146
Chapter 14	Our last goodbye	157
Chapter 15	The unknown	178
Lessons from Living with God		197
Teachings from Sananda		211

Living with God
Book 1
By Raven

A Year ago on the 12th of October 2005 I was being evicted from my home without a pot to pee in. Only my partner, my dog and our clothes were all I had left. A few of our chattels that we could carry were loaded into the car waiting to go.

The removal men had packed the remainder of our goods into a small container to go into storage.

I did not know how we were going to pay for that, but at least the removals company was happy to take the goods advising me that I could pay it sometime in the future.

The prophecy was coming true. I had always been told that I would end up in a lunatic asylum, prison, or on the streets, and at the age of 48 I felt that I was a complete disaster.

My life had been full of loss: two wives, many homes, countless failed business attempts, no friends and, worst of all, my beautiful 21 year old daughter, Emma, who had been crushed by a careless driver and had died in November 2003.

The judge in the local court house was becoming a well known face to me as mine was to him; I had been such a frequent visitor due to my business failures and marriage break downs. On each occasion that I had gone to court I ended up being told of my incompetence and having another layer of my material world stripped away from me.

I had worked so hard to create my security, self-esteem and success, and I had measured my life by the quality and amount of goods I had around me.

Little did I realise that I was the creator of all this disaster. I thought it was someone else's fault. I believed that the world was against me, that I carried the mark of villain like a tattoo on my forehead. I had nowhere to go. My creative mind was at a loss. In the past my quick thinking and workaholic attitude, coupled with my egotistical self-belief, had got me out of scrapes and managed to get me into yet another project that was going to save the world and create untold riches for myself.

Now I was empty, tired and unable see anything ahead of me.

What now?

I had tried everything I knew, and I didn't know how to succeed.

I GIVE UP! Whatever drives this world, whoever is in charge, I have had enough. I can't go on any more. Do what you will with me.

August the 8th 2006, marble floors, chandeliers, so many living rooms and bathrooms and of the highest quality - more than I could ever use. Not another house in sight. Just the sound of the house martins outside my window feeding the young in the nest. The complete peace and serenity I am experiencing here with my partner and dog in absolute luxury, surrounded by the most beautiful countryside: mountains, valleys, trees, rivers, all basking in the bright sunlight of this glorious Tuesday morning.

I have to pinch myself constantly to bring myself into my conscious mind to accept that this is the world that I am now living in. This is my home and my life. I do not have to worry about bills or debts or how we are going to feed ourselves or whether the car is going to keep going or not.

How the hell can this be?

I have not won the lottery or the pools. Nor have I come into an inheritance from a long lost relative and more importantly neither have I robbed a bank.

How can this be?

I have been given the opportunity of living with God, and I have taken it. God wants me to live in a far better way than I could ever choose for myself, and every day is filling my life with more and more abundance. This place I live in belongs to God and I am a happy guest.

ME...!! Living with God...!! Who would have imagined? And me actually using and saying the word 'God' without fear of judgement and ridicule let alone actually living with this power.

I realise now that since I have been living with God, my need to know how and why things have happened in order to control the outcome of everything because of my fear and insecurity, has disappeared from my being; I just know that everything is perfect.

I have detailed my experience of living with God for those who care to read it. I have also learned that I am only the messenger and have no control over what is said herein or happens to this or those who read it; other than that I know it will bring comfort, peace of mind and love to those who seek it.

"Something to understand is that we have been giving the same message since God made man and the world began. It never changes. We choose to deliver it in many different ways so that more people have the opportunity of getting the message, and we will continue to choose whatever medium we need to do so. We have not given any single person or group specific ownership of communicating God's word".

ᛤSANANDAᛦ

I have nothing new to teach the world.
Truth and non-violence are as old as the hills

Harijan, March 28, 1936

MK Gandhi

No matter which way it comes it has been said before, perhaps in a slightly different way. Nevertheless it has been said. The purpose for saying it in the way it is written in this book is for those who have not yet understood it. Simple messages clearly and honestly written still provide the greatest clarity and understanding.

Raven.

Chapter 1

Something had to give

I had often considered myself as different; hardly surprising with my track record! Everyone else that I had known had a job, car, house, family, pension etc.

I had none of these things.

On many occasions in my life I had turned to the great power in the sky to ask for help. It never came or so I thought. On July the 10th 2001 I finally accepted that I was so unhappy living the way I was. I sat back in the chair in my office gazing out of the window not focusing on anything. I allowed my mind to wander, drifting slowly back into my life, to the beginning.

I was born a catholic in the late 1950s and had spent much of my childhood in churches; or so it seemed. I would sit as an altar boy on the raised platform of the cavernous building dressed in my black cassock, grateful because it was so long that it came down to the floor hiding the holes in my shoes. The starched white tabard, which went over the top of the cassock, would cut into my neck, but the discomfort disappeared as I watched the people come in on a Sunday morning to ask for forgiveness for their transgressions of the past week. They would fill the pews from the back near the entrance so as not to have to walk the gauntlet of the staring judgemental eyes of the already seated waiting parishioners, and, more importantly, being closer to the exit meant a quicker escape.

The church that I went to was in the middle of a large catholic estate and held some 300+ parishioners. It was filled every time there was a service - for fear of excommunication if you failed to attend. However, this was not a place to hide in. The regular attending gossips would sit arms folded looking scornfully at some unfortunates who were that was the current talk of the estate, each of them self proclaimed judges nodding to each other and prodding the friend in front of them to point out the arrival of these lesser beings.

I could see, even then at the age of eight or nine, the kangaroo court in session in this revered house of God, something that I found amusing. It passed the time until the priest was ready to make his majestic entrance in silken robes that made him look regal, but right now he was peeping from his hiding place in the vestry at all the people he wanted to highlight in his sermon and some that he wished to lavish his thanks on; "For the lovely cakes she had made on his last visit" or to another for the great generosity that had been shown when they had given the considerable contribution of two shillings and sixpence to the desperately poor fund for the altar wine.

Living with God

    The new arrivals sat quietly. Their faces full of guilt, heads bowed to the floor hoping not to be seen by any person that had witnessed their sins, all hoping to get this over with quickly and get out, free to go, cleared of all wrongdoing again. Each of them would watch the minutes on the clock above the vestry tick away towards 12.00 noon as the sermon droned on and on, becoming impatient and fidgeting. Should the priest go past his allotted time for the service, the energy in the church would change markedly, as this was now their valuable drinking time being wasted. I often became amused as I felt the priest quicken his speech knowing that his last word would not be heard by half the congregation. This was the time that the bar opened in the catholic club in the grounds of the church, the barmen waiting to serve the repentant sinners who would come racing out of the double doors of the church, pushing past each other as the priest burbled his last sentence, up the hill to the club to be first in line to place their order for a drink, more alcohol. The alcohol would ease the guilt and smooth away the worries in the tormented minds of its drinkers.

    The catholic families of the 60s in the industrial midlands of England were large. Six to ten children per family on average. The homes were all controlled by the local priest who was always on hand to come to the house giving advice that created fear within the families he visited and which then translated into heavier alcohol use by the parents who handed their fear on to the children through the whole spectrum of abuse available to mankind.

    I had seen religion and hated it. God never existed in it for me, and I was still looking for something to save me from the hell I experienced as a child. Growing up in a family of eight surviving children from the sixteen that had been conceived by my parents was traumatic to say the least. Money, food, clothes and most of all love were in short supply; abuse of all kinds was no stranger to any of us. I was fortunate. A reprieve came for me when my life was in a state of deep confusion. I just could not relate to the friends that I had. Their lives were totally different from mine. They seemed to be experiencing everything that I did not and nothing of what I did experience.

On two occasions in my life I experienced what were to me very strange but fascinating moments. I had clinically died and on these occasions I had experienced what is now quite commonly known as an **out of body experience.**

To me this was a light that kept me alive!

I had seen things that were to help me survive the life that I was to lead.

I was given an understanding of why I was here on planet Earth and what I was to do on my journey, what life was about and where it was leading, but as a child it remained in my mind deeply lodged, never to be told to another human being for fear of being laughed at or considered completely mad. Had I considered talking to the priest or any other person of authority in my life about this, an exorcism would have been scheduled which would have been swiftly followed by banishment from the parish. I decided to keep it to myself because even *I* thought it was a dream.

It was only in later life that these experiences would come out of my mind where they had slept for so long and into my

Living with God

life as working tools that would help to create miraculous changes for me and some of the people in my life.

As I sat in my office reliving my childhood in my thoughts, I smiled as I recalled how many times I had sat and moaned to myself about my life and how bad it was. Why did it all happen to me? Why was his or her life better than mine? What was going on?

Countless, countless times!

I had done it so often when life was not quite the way that I wanted it to be. I was always looking for someone else to bail me out of my miserable existence.

I, like many, believed God to be beyond my grasp. My brain just could not get hold of the concept of this almighty power, who was benevolent, forgiving and all loving because this had not been my experience, and yet I knew there was something out there, because every time my life fell into crisis, something happened which brought about change for me. I had seen wonderful things happening to me in my out of body experiences and yet I was not experiencing changes that related to these events and the wonderful things I had seen. Life right now was just not panning out the way I needed it to.

Right now I was angry, miserable, living a life of being dishonest to myself, trying to get more through whatever means I could to shore up the ever increasing demand, not caring to some extent what I did to satisfy the growing needs of my family and my own hunger for material wealth and success. The need to earn more and more to stem the outgoing flow was growing out of control, and my need to please my family was far stronger than my ability to say no when I should have done. Coupled with my ego, that would not accept another defeat, my fear of failure and my inner emptiness made me feel like the living dead. Amazingly this continued for another two years.

The debt was out of control.

I was stretched to my limits. Something was going to break. The pressure that was building around the bills and debts that kept mounting up became like a nightmare that I was living 24 hrs a day. 2003 and I was now in my second marriage and had been for the last six years. I had not learned anything from my first marriage which had ended in disaster. My wife from my first marriage likened me to the devil and would see me dead in a flash, as she often told me. The only good thing that had come from that marriage was two beautiful daughters, one who was then in university and the other who had finished education and worked in the local government offices. I was more proud of them than I can ever express. I know that what they both achieved, which was considerable in both academic and personal arenas, was entirely due to their own commitment and perseverance. I had played no part in it.

My two daughters lived with their mother most of the time, apart from fairly regular occasions when they would have arguments with her and one or the other of my daughters would come and live with me until the dust settled and it was time to return to their own normality. I saw them frequently.

In my second marriage I had two stepdaughters, coincidentally they were exactly the same ages as my own daughters (was this God giving me another chance to see if

I could get it right second time around?). Their mother and I had been together since the girls were 10 and 11 years old. All four of the girls had meshed together from the start and were the best of friends, displaying a complete acceptance of each other as sisters.

In fact they were all delighted to acquire new siblings to grow up and share life with. It made the beginning of my second marriage very easy and great fun. We spent many hours together, all six of us, just happy to be in each other's company. All this had quickly faded as the girls grew and for the last four and a half years my second marriage had been only an existence. Whatever love there had been, had long gone and the relationship had broken down to a mutual tolerance of each other. I was certainly in need of help. My upbringing had led to a dysfunctional adulthood and I was growing increasingly incapable of handling life.

With a large mortgage to support a business with 20 staff, and a second business that was a distribution company that sucked my time and effort, I was unable to cope and it showed. Each area of my life was showing the signs of not getting my full attention and because of that, it was all falling apart at the seams.

I had started to tell my wife of our need to downsize our home and to curb our spending, but she and the girls had become accustomed to the life they were living, and every time I had the reply that I would manage somehow. I always pulled something out of the hat. I realised it was my own fault. Through my need to please, I had been the one to say, when times were tough in the earlier days, that we would manage, and in a sick way we had.

Raven

I had never been so unhappy in my life. (Now *that* is a powerful statement considering my upbringing). Then the bombshell hit me. Something had to give andin November 2003 something did give; something that would change my life forever.

Chapter 2

Emma

November 22nd 2003 my beautiful daughter Emma was killed.........

Emma was born on the 30th of June 1982. 7lbs, 12 oz, a tired little figure. She had taken the long route into the world; the birth process seemed to go on for days. I thought then and have done many times since, that this little spirit does not want to be here. She was fighting to stay in the comfort and safety of the womb, giving way finally to the forceps that dragged her into this busy world. Emma never seemed to grow physically. On many occasions throughout her early life we sought medical advice about this, only to be told that she was just petite and that there was nothing wrong with her.

I certainly recognised that it was only height that she lacked. Everything else, from her temper to her inquisitiveness was very normal. I took her to her first day in school at the age of four, dressed in her new school uniform. She looked like a little doll. All of her new classmates who were of a similar age with only months of difference between them were tiny, but Emma looked as if she was two years too early amongst them. Nothing about her size ever bothered her and she was well liked by everyone.

Her size also made no difference to her academic skills and she soared through her schooling with consistent effort.

I spent many hours with her talking of the spiritual world in which she displayed a great interest and in later years also sought and found great comfort. Emma finished her schooling with 8 or 9 High grade qualifications and decided - under pressure - to attend Bath University.

It was from her student accommodation that I got her call for help. She was desperately unhappy and asked me if she could come and live with me. She did not want to go on with this forced attendance at university and her mother had refused to allow her home if she left. I discussed it with my second wife, who agreed that we should go and get her. I will never forget the relief I saw on her face as she saw me arriving outside the property she was sharing with four other students. Her little one room accommodation said it all. She was so desperately unhappy there.

I packed her few belongings into the car and we drove to the university to cancel her place in the course she was attending. I felt her relief more and more as we severed the links with her unhappiness. As we drove away from the university I looked into the rear view mirror and saw her tears gently rolling down her cheeks as we silently drove home. As selfish as it may seem, this was the first time I had been able to be of fatherly service to my daughter for a very long time, and I was pleased that she had sought me out.

Emma was only with us for a short time, but before she had died, Emma and I went through a breakdown in our relationship. She had been living with my second wife, myself and my two stepdaughters. The room she shared with one of her stepsisters was small and cramped, and my wife had become increasingly grudging towards Emma, who was taking up the some of the valuable small space that had previously been her oldest daughter's alone, before Emma came to live with us.

The grudge in my wife had grown over weeks to the point of an explosion between the two of them. My wife complained to me about my daughter being lazy. Other unpleasant comments left me no alternative, and I sadly advised Emma that it would be best that she moved back to her mother's.

Emma left under a cloud with her boyfriend, who had come to collect her and her few sparse belongings. She hugged me and told me that she loved me, and the last words I spoke to her, were that I loved her and always would. I never saw her again or spoke to her. She was angry that I had not defended her against my wife, her stepmother.

The telephone call came out of the blue. I was at home with my wife and two stepdaughters when a call came that my wife answered. It was Emma's younger sister, my youngest daughter. She told my wife that she was with a policeman who had told her that Emma had been killed in a car accident. I saw the shock come over my wife's face as she heard the news. A momentary delay - then she screamed dropping the phone to the floor. She quickly recovered and told me the news. I was completely numb!

The next time I saw Emma was on the mortuary table. Her small body wrapped in a white cloth to hide the hideous damage. The only part of her on view was her head which was deformed from the impact of the truck that had killed her. The corpse was there, but I knew that my daughter had long gone. Sad at the sight of her body, I felt no overwhelming pain. Something told me that this death was not the end for Emma, only a new beginning.

I had nowhere to turn. I felt love and comfort from no one. I was completely alone in my grief. I was an outcast from my dead daughter's family. Emma's mother, my first wife, hated me with a vengeance, and at the funeral I was left at the back of the church, while my ex wife and her family and friends took up all other seating and room. I had been kept from having anything to do with my daughter's passing. I felt like a leper at her funeral. I felt the cold stares from faces that I knew and most that I did not. All the unknown faces seemed to have been briefed with a detailed account of what a terrible person I was, and what cheek I showed to turn up at Emma's funeral.

All I had to remember her by were the memories. I was disregarded and felt the pain so deeply. For me the end had finally come. I turned to God and said: "Whatever happens, I cannot live another day like this."

What was this? My life was a complete mess.

I got an answer!!!!!!!!!!!!!!!!!

I had an answer that shocked me - the type of response that I had never consciously had before. God actually spoke to me! (Was I going crazy or what?). Certainly my life was in such a mess. Perhaps I had gone crazy. After all in early life my parents and school teachers had told me that a mental institution or prison was probably where I would end up in later life.

Was this the beginning of that prophecy?

I was scared to think that they might have been right. After all everything was beginning to point that way. The writing was on the wall. Emma's death was just the start.

Chapter 3

The Good Doctor

For the last ten years I have cultivated a good close friendship with a man who I choose to call 'The Good Doctor' for the rest of this book - a title that this man earned with his tireless efforts to find answers where there were none and for his courageous open mindedness. He was a classically trained medical doctor who had finished his service with the N.H.S. as a consultant anaesthetist, finally deciding to leave a system he had worked in for many years in order to seek a path of healing others that was more suited to his beliefs.

He was a strong minded man full of the best intent for all that he met and worked with. A man that had vision and courage. Courage to face his peers and suggest that there could be another way. A less invasive way. A way that re-empowered people rather than dis-empowered them. He has joined the ranks of the medical people in the world that will be known in the future as the pioneers of their time. It will be said of him and his colleagues in time to come:

Living with God

"If only we had listened then instead of waiting so long!"

This is a statement that has been used in so many fields so many times before. Will we ever learn from our mistakes?

The Good Doctor became one of my best teachers and friends.

We had travelled the country together talking to audiences of various sizes, some as few as twelve, others in groups of hundreds. In fact, we talked to anyone who was interested in taking control of their own lives. We talked on matters mostly relating to female health issues, like the female menopause, p.m.s., breast cancer, uterine cancer, and numerous other diseases which he and I believed were all related to similar causes that could potentially be avoided with certain dietary and lifestyle changes.

Over our ten year friendship we had worked together on and off, but never on a full time basis exclusively together.

I guess we both knew that one day a purpose would bring us together on to a more permanent path.

Eventually it came; on the 12th of august 2002. The Good Doctor and his partner came to see me one evening out of the blue. His partner was a lovely gentle woman who openly enthused over her work and yet carried a reserved quietness that cloaked an incredible wisdom earned through many years of learning and experiencing. She also became another one of my best teachers.

We had been in relatively good close contact throughout the last year and on that evening, sitting in my kitchen, they asked me to come and help them to evolve their private health clinic. They needed my skills and knowledge combined with theirs to bring an idea they had into physical manifestation. I was excited and agreed to join them as a shareholding, managing director of this small concern. My career path had at one time been firmly fixed in the business field of small company development and finance. This had changed through another experience I underwent when talking one day with a woman who was suffering with breast cancer. She was a medium, who advised me that I was walking down the wrong path in life and needed to change. My real purpose was that of a communicator she told me (a very interesting story which I hope to share with you one day). As it happened I had wanted to find a new path in life for many years. I was quite unhappy with the dog eat dog world that I worked in and very bored with what I was doing. With this nudge from a complete stranger I decided to enter the field of nutrition in which I had a great interest along with other aspects of healthcare. Following years of training from some of the best teachers in the world, I stumbled into travelling the country and later the world teaching alternative healthcare to the interested medical profession and laypeople. I seemed to end up where the medium had told me I should be. (Coincidence? Perhaps not).

With The Good Doctor and his partner I became involved in establishing an alternative cancer treatment centre which was warmly welcomed by all the sufferers who found us.

So many people were in search of something else, or something that they could do to try to help themselves, while undergoing the treatment they were getting from the health service. We were amazed at the reception we got as we exploded this clinic into the waiting arms of so many. People were hungry for our services. The explosive growth of our clinic happened out of the sheer demand. This clinic was something we were able to create to support an overstretched, undervalued, under funded health service that was unable to provide what we could. Many more medical doctors became involved with us because they too wanted to find another way. Steeled by the courage of The Good Doctor who was showing them the way, they came to us in droves to learn.

We operated a service from The Good Doctor and his partner's private home developing from two staff to four and then quickly to another doctor and more nurses as the demand grew.

A mail order business grew alongside the clinic as the patients who had left our care went home and required more support. The clinic was thriving due to the epidemic that the world is still suffering from. Many new people were referred to us by happy visitors to our centre who had got better when they had had no hope before. We were quickly outgrowing our premises and needed to move.

Part of the treatment protocol we were using was a vitamin called B17, a naturally occurring plant cyanide which is non-toxic and has been shown to attack only cancer cells in the human body. It had been successfully used in a Mexican hospital under the management of two of the world's finest oncologists. The hospital doctors had cured 60,000 terminally ill patients since the hospital's inception in 1964 using this and other alternative techniques which we copied. One of those oncologists, a very successful author on the subject of alternative cancer treatments, became a frequent visitor to our small clinic giving advice to our staff and encouragement to the visiting patients.

The Good Doctor and I travelled to Mexico to spend time at the oncologists' hospital learning their techniques and the systems that worked so well. There is a strong body of thought that says that - at best - B17 has a placebo effect and at worst is poisonous, but we disagreed with that body. We spent many hours with the fifteen different medical consultants at the hospital seeing the actual results accumulated over many years. We studied this and other incredible God given substances taking the time to understand as much as we could about this amazing oasis that had grown in the desert of great need by so many. The evidence of the use of this type of treatment is overwhelming and available for those who wish to view it. I find it incredible; in fact, it beggars belief that such approaches to cancer treatments have had such little research time given to them by those that scorn its use. I ask the question, what are we afraid of finding? Perhaps something that may work? Or something that may threaten the multi billion dollar cancer business?

Within six months we were ready to move. We had found a building that would accommodate our staff which had grown to twenty and our ever growing need for more appropriate patient treatment space and better accommodation for handling the logistics involved in running our small company. It meant The Good Doctor, his partner and I taking up a hefty loan of £650,000.00 on a purchase price of 1 million pounds, which we all choked at. This fine Georgian building was perfect for our needs, and between us we managed to scrape together the difference between the loan and the purchase costs. We swallowed hard and signed personal guarantees and our own domestic properties over to the bank as security on the loan. We were nothing if not committed to our work.

People from all over the world came to our pioneering centre. We established good links with the local hospitals and Macmillan nurses. Oncologists from famous London hospitals referred patients to us that the health service was unable to support at that time. I became more and more involved in my work whilst my marriage was failing each day with alarming speed. It was pointed out to me by a close friend that I was becoming a workaholic. Suffering from a disease like this scared me, but not enough to do anything about it. Right now it served a purpose: I would rather be at work than at home. No love existed for me there. At least at work I was surrounded by the feeling of love - even if it was not for me.

Naively The Good Doctor and the rest of us carried on thinking that we had delivered a great service to mankind with our centre. It was to be short lived. We were growing fast and starting to become noticed by not so friendly forces.

We had always known that in England, as it is in most of the rest of the world, vitamin B17 is a controlled substance, meaning, the public can't get it unless it is prescribed by a medically qualified doctor, most of whom know little to nothing about it and therefore won't supply it. Apart from the fact that they are not allowed to whilst under the control of the Government health service, they risk loss of their ability to practice medicine if they are caught doing so.

We of course were not under National Health Service controls and therefore, as qualified medical doctors, our staff was entitled to prescribe and use this vitamin without concern.

We were then introduced to a very different world than the one we thought we lived in, a world that is not run on ethics or what is right, but a world that is run by money. I learned what goes on in the real world as they say and who is really running this world!

We were not in a controllable system like other systems that are devoid of the freedom of choice, and someone did not like it. We started to see all sorts of official bodies appearing out of nowhere, creating whatever rules they wanted to put us under to starve our small company into defeat. Using this substance vitamin B17 was no reason for stopping us, and they knew they couldn't so they used other tactics to make us submit.

It now seemed that my world was crashing down around me. That voice that spoke to me, that answer that I decided had come from God when I was at my wits end with Emma's death, took me back to the out of body experience I had as a child.

This was to help me now.

Chapter 4

The out of body experience

As a young boy growing up in a very harsh environment I had been considered a very sensitive child, prone to receding into myself and not being a great communicator of my feelings.

My siblings were very vocal and seemed to allow the things in life that happened to them to just float by, living each day as it came, accepting that they were powerless over what was happening to them, never considering why. I was far more interested in the whys and wherefores of these events. I wanted to know more about this world we lived in and to understand the purpose of being. Why did people do terrible things to each other?

I would find myself deep in thought and on more than one occasion in deep conversations with adults discussing the unexplainable.

"How do you know that what you see around you is not just created by a power greater than us for your own personal experience and that it really does not exist for anyone else?"

Questions like this posed by me, a small child, were often met with looks of incredulity; this kid is mad. I could see the thoughts of the listeners appearing in their eyes as though someone had just written them there. Just now and again I would meet someone who took my question seriously, and I watched the cogs of their brain churning away trying to figure it out, and I would sit enjoying the mental challenge I saw going on in them.

I was warmed by those people who were not completely closed to things that were beyond physical explanation, those who were open to considering: "Hey, what if that is right? How would that affect me and my world?"

When everything else in the world around me was too painful to dwell in, I could lose myself in deep thoughts that took me away from what was happening -even if only mentally. Locking myself into this world allowed me to escape the trauma that my body and emotions were suffering at the hands of my abusers. In here no one could get to me and own this part of my being. It was my safe haven and it has remained my sanctuary throughout my life.

Around the age of 7 or 8 years old I had been operated on in hospital to remove infected tonsils that had been causing me difficulty. After several days in hospital I had been sent home to continue my recovery. Late one night, soon after my arrival home, I suffered a haemorrhage in my throat and was rushed back to hospital. I was cared for by the doctors and nursing staff who repaired the damage and left me to sleep in a private room. I have no idea of time and space in what happened next, but sometime later that night when I was alone and all was quiet the haemorrhage started again, and in the quiet of the night I lay there choking without anyone knowing.

What happened to me was strange. I became conscious of myself floating above my body; I was looking down at myself for what seemed like an age. My body was still lying there in the hospital bed. I was just floating there feeling no pain or concerns. Just a little amused at what I was experiencing. A few moments later I became aware of pandemonium breaking loose as a nurse, who had come to check on me, raised the alarm that I had stopped breathing and was in danger. Lights, bells and bodies went off in all directions. I saw a crash team racing towards my bed with a trolley stacked with multi-fangled equipment. As this commotion continued with the team going through crash procedure on my inert body, I became aware of something else happening to the floating energy that was me.

(This is really stretching my nerves writing down this information that has remained God's and my secret for so long. I keep looking round as I write this expecting to see men coming down the path with a straitjacket).

I had left my body and now turned away from the commotion in the hospital room as I started to travel through a dark tunnel. The tunnel felt really weird as I started to move along it feeling a little perturbed but not frightened. I could see a bright light at the end of it. The further down it I went, the more aware I became of the feelings of complete peace and serenity that was descending over me. No pain, no needs, no concerns, no fears. I felt only the feeling that comes with the warmth of receiving unconditional love. Something that was then completely new to me.

This for me was the first time I had ever felt love, and so I was enjoying every blissful moment of the journey down that tunnel which did not seem to take more than a few minutes.

As I left the tunnel and came into the light, I was greeted by the images of all the family that I had known and some of them that I had not while being alive. My young cousin Margaret who had died about the age of 8 or 9yrs, my grandparents who I had not known and other family members. All of them were smiling, happy to see me cheering and clapping. It was as though I had just won the London marathon.

I looked beyond this group to see a figure standing behind a gate inside a beautiful garden. The figure beckoned me forward. As I got closer I realised that this figure was Jesus dressed in brilliant white robes. I guessed it was him from pictures that I had seen in church and at school. He was warm and smiling, loving and happy to see me. It felt so good!

In my passing from life to the first stages of death God and I had agreed that Jesus was the physical form that would be presented to me. I was not consciously aware that I had made this agreement, but I have since learned my consciousness goes beyond the physical limitations of my brain. Jesus was a figure that I was familiar with and able to feel comfortable with. Jesus was the representative of God that had come to meet me. I know that now.

Jesus motioned me through the gate, and as I entered standing beside him as tall as his waist, I looked up into his eyes as he put his arm around me. I had never been held like this in my short life, and for the first time ever I felt completely safe.

We walked through the garden and talked of many things. We talked of my life that had already been, of the future and of other things that for now are not relevant to this story.

Our conversation came to an end on the discussion of what was to happen now. Jesus explained to me that I was to return - that my life was to continue. I had many things to accomplish, and I would be protected on my journey. I complained bitterly. I did not want to leave. I did not want to go back to the abuse and poverty I was experiencing in the life I had chosen to live.

This place with Jesus was heaven in every respect of the word. I gave one last bleat of discontentment at having to return, and as I looked into his eyes I knew that I had to go back to carry on my life.

Jesus hugged me into his robes and held me for a few moments. Those precious moments have lived with me ever since. He then ushered me through the gate into the waiting hands of a guide that was to stay with me throughout the rest of my life journey. I was surprised to be met by a red Indian in full regalia. He was powerful - yet to me felt kind and gentle.

Later I was to know this Indian and his comfort and help far better. I have never forgotten the voice and words of Jesus, or the look of knowing and love that I saw in his eyes. It has carried me through the most difficult times on my journey. I felt myself quickly returning down the tunnel. A feeling of sadness was on me to leave such love and comfort, but I now knew why I had to return and I accepted it.

I believe that this brief respite from my life as a child was God's intervention; it was enough to give me a breathing space to have a chance of completing this life journey. Without it I would truly never have made it. I knew then, that there was more than just this human existence. There was an opportunity. My moment of respite was giving me a leg up to taking advantage of this opportunity.

This and other experiences were the things that just kept me hanging on to the hope that something else existed. This memory returned as I felt my world crumbling around me.

On January 2004 the same voice I had heard in the garden, the voice I had heard when I had asked for help when Emma died, spoke to me again.

Are you sure that you are ready to give up?

I had never been so sure in my life. The thought of trying to continue in the way that I had been living my life, left me feeling like I would rather die now.

I am sure.

Then leave everything and follow me!

What do you mean leave everything?

Leave everything that you posses, your home, your business, your family, your life and follow me!

I felt gripped with fear and excitement. Was this for real? What the hell? I kept that message in my mind contemplating the words that I had heard, but doing nothing more about it.

Chapter 5

The reunion with Emma

Out of the blue I went to see a friend of mine who had contacted me saying that he wished to channel spirit for me, to give me a message, some guidance. I had known this man for some time and had been involved with some of his work before, although I had kept my own council on how much of it I believed. With a certain amount of reservation I went to see him.

My experience of the past told me that we are not alone; something exists which is far greater than we are, but I had not contemplated looking to this power with any real confidence, expecting that doing so couldn't change my life.

It was January 2004 and I was still feeling very bruised from the loss of my daughter and all that went with it.

On arriving at my friend's home I was ushered into a room which was furnished with two cushions and nothing else. It felt cold and empty, and I was feeling very much that this was a waste of time, unsure if I believed any of it.

My friend entered the room after some time and sat down in front of me. He is American and is a very large powerfully built man who can be quite overwhelming in his presence.

I sat and looked into his eyes feeling very hurt in my grief and feeling sceptical. What followed shocked me to my boots. As we sat looking at each other in complete silence without moving, this giant of a man burst into tears, and the following words gushed from his mouth,

"I am so sorry that I have been such a cold hearted bitch, Daddy"

I was stunned. These were my daughter's words. The words that she had used in life. These words quickly dissolved any immediate doubt that she and I were communicating.

Now, here was Emma sitting here in front of me talking to me through my friend's body. After the initial shock I accepted that this was my daughter.

My friend had never met my daughter and certainly would not have known of our relationship difficulties towards the end of her life. He could not have just conjured up the words that she would have used, when she was alive.

Emma and I relaxed into a smooth conversation. We talked of her life, of our love for each other as a father and a daughter, and of where she was now. She described to me the place where she was. It was the same place where I had been as a child, when I had gone through the out of body experiences. Something that I had never told her, when she was alive.

She told me of the stages that she had been going through, since she had died and reviewed her life and experience. She was now with a man who had been helping her through this journey since death. He was a kind, helpful man, and she was happy and safe with him. Finally she told me that I should now carry on with my life in the knowledge that she was in a good place. She had decided to go with this man now into the final stages of her death and rebirth, and she was very happy. I was not to worry about her any more.

At that we said our final goodbye and hugged each other. Then she left.

My friend and I were silent for a long time. I was trying to take in all that had just happened - fighting the scepticism and weighing up whether this had all been a hoax or not.

I thought the session with my friend had come to an end, and I started to thank him. I was shocked again when a voice said: "*We have not yet left.*" This was the voice I had heard from my childhood experience - the voice I had heard recently when I turned to God saying "I give up." It was the voice of the man that Emma had described to me a few moments ago - guiding her and loving her. It was Jesus.

He spoke to me again of my request for help: *Are you ready to give up everything and follow me?*

We talked of many things, until the conversation came to an end, and I was to follow the instructions given, if I wanted the help I had asked for.

The session with my friend was over. He came back into his own body and into his own consciousness.

We talked about what had happened in brief. I thanked him and we parted company. He had someone else to see. I went and sat in the garden of his home by the river. I was still in a daze; my mind racing to try to put all that had happened into some sort of box that made it acceptable within the boundaries of reality that I understood - the boundaries by which I had lived my life, trying to find some logical process to explain what had happened.

I couldn't.

I finally came to accept that everything was exactly as it had happened.

I became aware that a feeling of complete peace had descended over me. I no longer felt pain around Emma's death, or blame for the one who killed her. I could now celebrate her life and start to rejoice her death, because in her dying she had gifted me, and everyone she had touched in her short life, with an opportunity of learning and understanding that the only thing that is of value in this world, is the relationships we have with each other and the quality of them.

To recognise that love is all that matters.

My material life struggle had come to an end.

My struggle for recognition was over.

This was the most valuable lesson I have ever had, but also the most expensive one.

One year later I visited the courthouse, where the young man who had caused her death was being sentenced. I had not been to any of the previous hearings. I felt that doing so would only continue the pain of her loss. I was powerless over the outcome of the court hearing and accepted that the judicial system would do as it saw fit. Sitting listening to how and why the whole event happened would only cause me more pain than I had already felt, and my heart had cried enough.

On arriving at the courtroom my daughter's mother and her entire family were sat in the public gallery. All were dressed in black suits looking angry and bitter. As I entered the quiet room all eyes turned to me in my jeans and casual shirt. I felt the venom towards me from my ex-family.

I took a seat behind this group and sat to hear the proceedings.

To my left, in a separate box, escorted by prison officers, sat the lonely young man who had been involved in this terrible accident. Behind me sat his mother, father, brother and pregnant girlfriend all sobbing.

I watched the proceedings without really listening. From time to time I observed the side glances from my first wife and members of her family towards this young man. The looks were cold and could have frozen petrol with the amount of anger and blame they contained.

The young man was sentenced to eighteen months in prison which meant he would be free in one year with good behaviour. At the announcement of the sentence the group in front of me roared with anger demanding a longer sentence, and that it was a crime to let him go so lightly.

We were all ushered out of the courtroom. The family of the sentenced going into a side room with their lawyer, and my ex-wife and her group going into another making a great commotion.

I followed the sentenced young man's family into the side room. It was very small and cramped. As the door was closed by the lawyer behind me, they all realised that I was with

Living with God

them, but none of them knew who I was. The Lawyer asked. The whole family were in tears and looked up as this question came. I could see the fear in their eyes as I told them I was the father of Emma. They huddled together expecting anger, and the lawyer stepped forward also concerned that I had come to seek revenge.

I said in a quiet calm voice that I wished them to pass on a message to their son who had been escorted off to the cells below the courthouse ready to begin his sentence. I paused to wait for their agreement. The silence was deafening. All were expecting threats. I simply said that Emma was now dead and nothing could change that. Accidents, and this was an accident, do happen. This young man had fallen asleep behind the wheel of his truck, and the truck had veered across the road and crushed my daughter.

None of us is free from the possibility of being involved in something as tragic as this.

The lawyer told me that the young man had attempted suicide twice since the accident had occurred. I continued and said to please tell him that I forgave him, and that he should now try to put this terrible event behind him, to pray for Emma and look towards his future with his girlfriend and the child she was carrying.

They all looked at me stunned as I thanked them for their time and left the small room. I felt another level of freedom and peace come over me as I walked down the stairs out of the courthouse.

Outside on the pavement stood Emma's mother and her group surrounded by newspaper reporters and photographers. As I walked past them the cries of injustice were being repeated over and over by the group. Cameras were flashing and I walked quietly away from the hustle. For me it was all over.

Leave everything and follow me!

These words rang in my head again as I walked away. What I had done was part of my instructions from God. I was now free of this event entirely, and as I looked back I realised the wisdom of these words that were ringing in my ears. God did not mean me just to leave behind the material things of life, but also these events that become for most of us a millstone around our necks that we carry to the grave, and in most cases they speed up the journey to the grave.

As I looked back I saw the millstone of this event being placed upon the shoulders of all those that were choosing to carry it. The clouds were gathering around them; great storm clouds of grief and anger. I felt sorry for them all for the first time in my life, and totally out of the blue, in total contrast to anything I had ever done before, I prayed for them. For me the whole saga was over. I was free of all the pain surrounding Emma's death.

Chapter 6

Leave everything and follow me

Following my meeting with my daughter and God through my friend's body I knew that my life had now changed forever. Any doubt that God existed was over, and following those simple words was the beginning of my freedom from myself and everything that was painful in my life.

My view on religion had not changed since a child, I disliked it intensely, but since all the events that had taken place I had started to listen to this voice and accept that I was being given guidance from something more powerful than me.

It takes courage to follow your heart!

By now I was aware that I could no longer stay in the marriage I was in or continue in my present life. It was too painful. I could not live another day without love. My daughter's death had taught me this, and I knew that love did not exist where I was. Staying in the marriage would only continue the act! Of being happy.

To everybody outside everything looked rosy. Three cars on the drive, five bedroom house, two apparently successful businesses, three daughters doing well in university, a wife who appeared happy. What more could anyone wish for?

I was dead inside! Emotionally bankrupt.

It takes courage to follow your heart! Leave everything and follow me.

God was saying this to me again and again. I felt the fear rise in me, as I kept hearing those words. Then another bombshell hit me,

---

To stay in a marriage that does not have respect and love is to live a lie to God, this woman and yourself. Get out!

Get out! I thought it was a sin to leave a marriage? You know, vows to you and all that....

Vows to each other. Not us! Get out!

I had lived a life of certainties, or so, I thought.

Living with God

Fear had played such a big role in my life that I never did anything unless I was certain of the outcome of the next thing I was going to do or where I was going to go.

I was being told to get out of my marriage without any knowledge of what would befall me. I stood shaking inside, sweating, feeling nausea and afraid of how I could get out of this.

For days I contemplated this message, and I continued to work, with the purpose of staying away from home, as I could not bear to be there.

I was flying all over the world giving health lectures and striking deals on supplies for our cancer centre. Working like a dog had become my distraction from myself. If I kept myself busy enough and so tired from working, I did not have to face the inevitable.

Following a four day trip to Texas where I had been working, I decided that I could no longer procrastinate on the words I had heard from God. I had to do something. While I had been on the trip, I had been talking with two mutual female friends of my wife and I. We had been talking about life and relationships in general. These discussions had cemented for me the knowledge that I was living a lie in virtually all areas of my life, and I had to clean it up. Neither of these women then knew the importance or the impact that these discussions were going to have in my life, but I thank them now for their honesty.

On returning home I confronted myself and told my wife that I was leaving her. I have never felt so afraid in my life. I have often since thought about why I had felt such fear from that situation. I had been sexually, mentally and physically abused as a child, shot at while on active duty in the British army, my whole body set on fire in a petrol incident, run down by a car and comatose in hospital for a week. None of these things created the terror in me that I now felt telling my wife it was over. I realise now that I had allowed myself to become part of a co-dependent relationship, a relationship that was full of abuse in so many ways that I had become a child again, afraid to be me. My wife was a powerful highly intelligent woman and I found it difficult to match her speed of mind and command of vocabulary which often left me twisted in knots.

I stood shaking in the bedroom with my back against the wall as I told her. I was as white as a sheet. She stood on the other side of the bed telling me that I was wrong and that that was not what I wanted. She knew better. I started to see the madness of my life. She started to feel the fear gripping her with the realisation of what was happening, turning white and becoming even angrier. In the past she had managed to override my cries for change with her powerful verbal control. I had to fight that control now by making the statement again and again that it was over, and that I was leaving. Finally I left the house like a scared rabbit not knowing where I was going, or what I would do. With no clothes or anything else I drove away.

I had followed God's words. What the hell now?

I ended up staying with a friend and his family in Bristol. Alone I stayed in a room and talked with God for days ignoring the constant flow of calls and texts from my wife wanting to know where I was and telling me that I had better come back. I was afraid, but the conversations I was having with God calmed me.

Have faith and know that in handing yourself to me I will not forsake you.

For me this was the biggest test of my life. Up until now I had not trusted anyone or anything.

Chapter 7

Meeting the Angel

Then the lessons began and with them a whole new journey.

Throughout a lifetime of abuse I had learned to rely only on myself. That was a big mistake. God taught me that my life journey so far had contained such abnormal experiences that through them I had learned to become dysfunctional. The relationships with my parents and now two wives had all been abusive and as a by product I had become lost.

I was unable to function as a normal human being. (If you had asked Me, I was perfect, would have been my answer)

In the past I had always been able to point the finger at others. It was someone else's fault as to why my life was rat shit. I had had so many negative experiences in my life, things that had happened to me, a veritable armoury of excuses for why things went wrong, or why I was demonstrating my bad behaviour, negative attitudes, jealousy, control, and even my ego. I could blame it all on something or someone else except myself, and I had spent a lifetime doing it.

Now I had accepted that God existed and was here to help me; the change could begin. My life could become better. I was expecting a lottery win. Not so!

My ego started to be shown to me. How I cringed and squirmed as God took me through some of the events of my life: The people I had hurt, the awful things I had done. I realised how much I had hidden from myself, and I wanted to curl up and hide. I was full of jealousy, anger and control. I was self- centred and full of fear.

I sat in that room in my friend's house in Bristol. and Jesus came to me again standing beside me as the events of my life unfurled in front of me like a tortuous film.

This was a personal Christmas Carol.

I was shown all of these events with my part in them being highlighted and standing out to me like a lighthouse on a stormy winters night. I saw myself for the first time in my life. I came to know who and what I had become, and I WAS ASHAMED.

At the end of this experience, and after several days of allowing myself to feel all that had been shown to me, I felt another level of peace come over me. I had begun to accept myself warts and all. Just like scrooge I had a chance to put things right, though this was not to consist of buying people turkeys and turning up to parties to start taking part in relatives' lives as he had. It meant starting to change within myself. Starting to live a new life with my new guide, God! I was still not sure what this meant, but I was becoming more accustomed to the thought of doing so.

After staying with my friends and going through this experience, it was time to leave them and start clearing up some of the debris of my life. I left their home and started the drive back towards Salisbury. I switched on my mobile phone as I drove, and the phone started to vibrate continuously with the barrage of messages that my wife had left on the phone. Before it could stop receiving all the messages, the phone rang. It was her. I felt the fear immediately as she started to berate me on the phone. This was madness. I felt like I was on the run from my own wife. Was this how normal relationships were or how they became?

The only way I could stop her was to agree to return home. On arriving we sat and started to talk. She was convinced that I had someone else, that I was having an affair. She was not prepared to accept that I was leaving her because I needed to experience love and that it did not exist for me in our relationship.

I realise now that my family was completely co-dependent and by me following God's guidance, it would bring about a healing in my whole family.

After talking for some time it was apparent to my wife that I was not going to change my mind. My brief respite period at my friend's house in Bristol had given me a stronger resolve. I was not going to return to the existence of the past no matter what happened.

We finally agreed that it would be best for me to leave permanently. I packed some clothes and left. The messages and phone calls stopped.

I had agreed with my friends, The Good Doctor and his partner, that I would stay in their house while I found myself

Living with God

alternative accommodation. The house was in the country, so I spent much time walking in the woods feeling the relief of being apart from my wife.

It was a freedom that I had never felt before. I was starting to breathe, starting to feel alive for the first time; I was noticing things around me, the beauty of nature, the wind and the sunshine. I felt like I had just been released from a forty six year prison sentence. I had not just left my wife. I had left my life.

I was in awe of my surroundings I had missed so much.

Here I was living in one room with less material security than I had ever had, and I felt more freedom than at any other time in my life. I was starting to feel comfortable in my own skin becoming accustomed to who and what I was.

I began to like my life. I spent much of my time talking with God. I was still not aware of what was in store for me. Fear still played a big role in my life. I had followed the guidance, and sure I was feeling all these new and wonderful things, but was this it? Living alone in one room, walking in the woods, seeing nature, waiting. What was I to do next? Impatience had been the bane of my life.

I have since learned that as soon as I take the courage to let go of something, it is soon replaced with something much better. God's choices for me far exceed what I would give myself. I have also learned that sometimes the gifts from God do not appear to be gifts that I like, but my experience shows me that they are always what I need!

I had let go of my family, told God that I wanted to experience love and now I was. I was feeling the love that is embodied in all the things that in the past I had not even noticed. But I wanted to experience physical love!

Let go of everything and follow me!

Here it was again. The same statement again. I had let go of my marriage. What was I to let go of now?

Materialism!

Back at work in our clinic I decided to follow this advice a little further. I was going to hand to my wife the distribution business that I had started. It was thriving and had promise of being something very large. Its growth had become self-perpetuating and to let it go was a struggle for me.

I called my wife and told her of my decision and wrote a letter which gave her sole ownership of the business. She would have enough income to sustain a good lifestyle and, if carefully managed, a secure financial future.

This was pushing my buttons.

Ok, God. How about that?

Not a bad start!

This was becoming fun! in a weird sort of way! I was sensing greater depths of freedom the more I let go.

All of the people I worked with in the clinic were what I call spiritual types. Not religious, but kind, gentle and full of the best intent towards mankind.

Living with God

One morning while talking to my friend, The Good Doctor, he sensed the stress in my voice and suggested that I asked one of the staff to give me a healing. This type of healing called Reiki was common in our clinic; non invasive, and pretty much all our staff were practitioners of this, including all of the doctors and nurses. I agreed that it might do me some good. I was tired and stretched.

We finished our conversation, and I continued working with the mundane day to day events of the centre. Later in the morning I felt that what The Good Doctor had advised me would be a good idea, and I opened my office door with the intention of asking the next member of staff that passed to give me a healing.

The next person that passed was a young woman who I knew very little. She had been working at our centre, and I had not really spoken with her since her interview with me some 6 months earlier.

She was 29 years old and had come to us on the recommendation of one of our nurses. She was not a nurse, but the one who had recommended her, had said that we would be wise to see her. I had learned that ignoring this type of advice could sometimes be a big mistake, and what was I to lose from seeing her?

On the day of her interview we were looking for another nurse to help with the increasing workload. A very well qualified young woman had come on the same day, and I had decided to employ her. Now what was I to do with this other young woman who was not qualified to do what I was looking for and quite frankly did not have a need for? I felt something compelling me to offer this young woman a position nevertheless.

She had a sparkle, something special. What it was I did not know, but I knew there was a purpose for her being with us. The position was to be part time, and it would be a menial position cleaning toilets, making tea and clearing up. She accepted without batting an eye and decided to stay on for the rest of the day to become acquainted with the centre and the rest of the staff. I had not noticed her again since then. This woman had just slotted into the clinic, and I had never really seen her again until now.

As she passed my door I called her and asked for a healing. She was surprised at my request as I had hardly ever spoken or had anything to do with her. She readily agreed and arranged to meet me in one of the treatment rooms in 30 minutes.

I finished what I was doing and went to the treatment room. The room she had chosen to see me in was once a bedroom in this grand old Georgian house which had been painted in a bright but warm calming orange colour. It was empty apart from a healing couch in the centre of the room and a chair in one corner next to a small table that held the small CD music player. She was sitting beside it waiting for me. She beckoned me on to the healing couch. I kicked off my shoes and (for some reason) feeling very nervous I lay down closing my eyes.

A very gentle background music was playing in the room. She covered me with a blanket, and I soon drifted off falling into a dream state while still conscious of this woman and my surroundings.

I started to feel the presence of other energy invoked by the music that was playing, all the creativity of my fertile mind wanting to believe anything other than what I had known in life, a red Indian standing close, angels at my head and feet giving me a feeling of security and comfort, I felt myself being held spiritually and comforted like a small baby, without touching my body, I felt the energy of this young woman close to me, as her hands came over my chest hovering above me I was aware of a feeling that her hands had reached into my body and were holding my weary heart. I was overcome with a feeling of deep love. I cried more than I had ever been able to in the past.

After what seemed like an age the healing came to an end, and I lay there for some time not wanting to move from the pleasure of my experience. I felt more and more conscious of the woman sitting in the corner waiting for me to return. I opened my eyes and looked at her as she stood and came towards me. I sat up and she asked if it was o.k. to hug me. I agreed and as she wrapped her arms around me. My head exploded into confusion. What was happening to me? I felt overwhelming **love** towards this young woman who I hardly knew.

She stood back from me, my mind was reluctant to let go of her. She proceeded to tell me that during the healing she had seen me as a child, had seen that I had never experienced love, even as a baby. She told me things she had seen describing the clothes I had been wearing, what age I was, where I was.

Raven

Another shock hit me; this woman was seeing into my past. My soul had been exposed to her, which made me feel extremely vulnerable.

I thanked her and ran out of the treatment room to my office as fast as I could. I needed the safety of my own surroundings. Closing the door behind me I fell into my chair sitting in bewildered amazement at what had just happened.

How could I feel such a deep love for this woman, this woman I hardly knew, a woman so much younger than me, living in such a different world to me? God had sent a living angel to me, and I had in an instant fallen in love with her.

I spent the rest of the day in a state of confusion trying to get on with work, but with my mind continuously going back to the events of the morning.

This could not happen. Was I going mad?

At the end of the day as all the staff were leaving, the young woman came back to my office knocking quietly on the door which was open. I turned to her and felt my heart jump into my throat. Dry mouthed I tried to speak, but nothing came out. She looked gently into my eyes. I was sure she could see the fear in me.

"I have received guidance to offer you another healing tomorrow if you would like to consider having it", she said.

Such was the power of my feelings towards her now that I wanted to be close to her at any opportunity I could grasp rightly or wrongly. I could not help my feelings. Aware that I was her employer and this was wrong, what I was feeling was not allowable in the workplace, I would be breaking every rule in the book, I would be lying and my reason for accepting the healing would be wrong. I accepted I was not interested in the healing now, I just wanted to be near her, to feel the cool gentleness of her presence.

I watched her leaving the building. Was she aware of how I was feeling?

Could she be feeling the same as me?

How ridiculous was I even to think that? This was a beautiful young woman. I watched her walk through the grounds of the clinic towards the one bedroom cottage that she shared with her boyfriend; her boyfriend, our gardener Patrick, a man of Irish decent who had lived his life in London. Very streetwise. Powerfully built. A man that left you feeling that he would take no prisoners should he be riled. Another good reason why my mind was playing with fire. I had to let go of this ridiculous thought, the thought of me being with her.

That night was sleepless. I concluded in the ramblings of my mind to put these silly thoughts out and to get on with my life. But God saw things differently from me.

The next day I toyed with not going into the office. I had to let go of the events of the previous day and get back to reality, Nothing good could come from yesterday. I have also since learned that whatever God wants to happen, it will happen. Neither I nor anyone else has power over it.

During the previous night I had spent time asking God to relieve me of the pain I was feeling, the pain of knowing that this love was not to be and not to torture me with what I would never be allowed to experience. But instead I had not been able to stop myself from going into work. Instead of feeling relief from my pain it was increasing.

Raven

The allotted time for the next healing came, and the young woman came to my office to ask me if I was ready. I opened my mouth to say that I wished to cancel it, but the words that came out were different.

"I am ready!"

I was completely powerless.

God was driving and I was a powerless passenger. Every fibre of my being was screaming to stop, but I was forced to go on. I told her that I would be with her in a few minutes, and she left to prepare.

I sat and said "God, please. Tell me what is happening."

Love is happening. The love that you asked for. The love that you have craved for all your life. The love that is available to all mankind. The love from whence you came and the love to which you will return is available to you now on Earth. Allow it to be. Accept it with an open heart.

I gave in. I accepted that whatever God had in store for me would be better than my choices had been. I let go and trusted.

Leaving my office I felt peace and acceptance. Full of nervous energy I walked through the building to the treatment room. Other members of staff were passing me talking and asking questions, but I was in another world, and I just passed them in a daze not speaking or answering them. As I entered the treatment room which was full of light, I immediately

Living with God

became aware of the gentle music playing in the background. I felt my lungs seize, unable to breathe as I saw her standing in the middle of the room. She was tall and elegant with long chestnut hair cascading over her shoulders.(olive coloured skin), her face aglow with deeply loving blue eyes staring out towards me. Her look was drawing me towards her. I felt hypnotised, unable to stop whatever was happening.

She beckoned me to a single chair in the middle of the room, and I sat closing my eyes. The room was filled with incense which was adding to my headiness. I could smell the sweet freshness of her close to me, and I fell again into the bliss of her energy.

I could have died happy in that moment. This was the same bliss that I had felt in my near death experiences as a child, the same bliss I felt sitting talking with Jesus and God. I was in the presence and power of this angel.

The healing that took place this time was a different type of healing to the one I had experienced the day before. I could feel this goddess moving around me, making motions with her hands around my head and shoulders. At times I felt her hands gently resting on my head so gentle and yet powerful. Just to feel these beautiful hands touching my head sent a charge of electricity through my body. I was in heaven.

At the end of this ceremony I was stood up with my eyes closed and my arms folded across my chest. She wrapped her arms around me again and whispered into my ear

"You have received the sword of Archangel Michael, the sword of truth and the cup of love from Archea Faith. Welcome!"

Then another bombshell, "It is o.k. to love now", she whispered in my ear!

I had never loved or been loved in my life. What was this angel saying to me? Did she mean it was o.k. to love her?

The confusion again!

I was reeling from this message, falling out of control. I ran again to my office, and she followed moments behind me, closing the door behind her.

She was aware that something had happened to me and asked what I had experienced in the healing. I was panicking. How could I tell her? I was back in the world that said this could not be!

All sense of right and wrong left me!

God took over. I leant forward towards her cupped her beautiful face in my hands. Her eyes were deep pools of love, and I readily dove into them. I kissed her gently on the cheek and told her that I loved her.

As I stepped back, the shock of what had just happened came over her face. Panicked, she ran from my room, and I was left standing in the middle of the floor, too stunned to move.

What had I done? I felt such a fool. I had been unable to control myself, and now I had caused this angel deep hurt by overstepping the boundaries of acceptable behaviour in the workplace or outside it for that matter.

What was to happen now?

I was partly ashamed for my actions and partly accepting of them. I was in love, bursting at the seems, and even at the risk of shame, humiliation and a damn good thumping from her boyfriend. I relaxed into the acceptance of the love

I felt in my heart. Whatever the outcome of all this was to be, I could never and would never ever again deny myself love or my true feelings. I only hoped that from here on I would act in a responsible and acceptable way.

What am I saying for crying out loud? Love knows no boundaries when it happens. We have no control over it happening, but I was now praying that my outburst had not hurt her or anyone else that may be connected to all this.

All I could do now was await the repercussions.

While sitting in my office in a state of what I can only describe as nothingness, she came back and told me that I was wrong to kiss her and left as abruptly as she had arrived.

I had seen the panic that had been created, etched on her face as if carved with a chisel. I felt lost, alone and in pain, a deep pain that was crushing my very soul. I watched her for days after, becoming more aware of her other qualities. She was acting as if nothing had ever happened. I saw her kindness and gentleness towards everyone she encountered, her complete honesty. I watched her playing in the gardens during her lunch breaks, cart wheeling like a child without a care. Her sense of play and fun was very endearing and brought happiness to a place that was often filled with people facing death. I soon realised that this woman who had started cleaning toilets six months earlier had become a source of life to our centre. She was the one that those who were in pain sought out. She comforted the dying and the families. She was able to create healing in people that medicine had no concept of how to heal.

Raven

She became the voice of reassurance to staff and patients alike. Had I just stupidly taken all of what she was to everyone and fallen in love with it?

Going in to work was becoming an effort that I could not bear; to see this angel and not be with her, was more than I could take. I started to spend more time away. If I was not around her perhaps this would all die away. It didn't.

On a Saturday morning several weeks later the staff had arranged a barbeque in the gardens of the clinic when we had no patients.

The work was hard and often the team could get together to have some relaxation time as a group. I was away on one of my jaunts when I received a phone call from The Good Doctor telling me of the event, and that all the staff wanted me to come. I was not aware that any of them knew of my feelings towards the angel that worked there. After much persuasion I agreed to go.

On arriving I crept quietly into the centre's car park. Everyone was in the garden at the back of the clinic, and I could hear the laughter and music, smell the food cooking and hear children of the staff running around. I stood next to my car, I want too run away. I was still in the deep pain of love.

I started to get back into my car when one of the staff saw me and came running out catching my arm and dragging me towards the party. I was in so much pain that I found it difficult to smile. I was in no mood to be a part of this. After talking politely to some of the team, I noticed the angel looking at me from another group gathered on the lawn. They were all chatting and laughing with each other. The angel was involved in the fun but kept looking towards me with those gentle, loving eyes.

It was more than I could take. I made my way through the building towards the main exit on the other side of the clinic. I gave my apologies to my friend The Good Doctor, making excuses that I had urgent things to attend to and left through the main door.

As I was walking down the steps the tears were welling in my eyes, how could I ever carry on like this?

She called me from the top of the stairs, "Are you leaving?"

"Yes. "

"Why?"

"I have things to attend to," I lied!

"Please stay. I want you to stay."

I walked back into the building with her and asked her to come with me into an office away from the crowd.

As we entered The Good Doctor's consulting room I closed the door behind us. We were alone. No noise, no interruptions. I had to tell her why I could not stay. It was burning in my chest like a firecracker exploding.

"I am in love with you and I cannot bear to be here. It hurts too much to see you, be near you, and not hold you in my arms."

"I have to go."

The angel took my hands and held them gently. "Please don't go!"

I could not refuse her anything; she wanted me to stay even knowing what I had just told her.

Raven

I would have laid my life down for her. How could I refuse to stay? I was powerless over this love!

The days passed, and the energy between us started to grow as we became great friends. Other people in the centre became aware of the energy and started to become suspicious of this closeness. We talked with each other as often as we could. She told me that when she had given me the first healing, she had felt a near uncontrollable urge to kiss me. This had never happened to her before or since. She told me that she had always been aware of my presence whenever I entered a room. She knew it was me without even looking. She told me that although she had not been conscious of any attraction towards me, she could not now deny that she was falling in love with me. She had felt the same explosion in the healing that I had.

How could all of this turn into something positive? I was still married although separated and she was in a long term relationship.

It was not for us to do anything. God had decided on this relationship. As much as we tried to deny this love the more it grew. Unable to be together or expand our feelings into actions we had to wait for God's intervention.

It came some days later. On a phone call between us we talked about our situation and came to no conclusions on how it could be resolved. We ended the phone call on a sad note. I was resigned to the fact that perhaps it would never be anything more than a close friendship.

I went into work on a morning shortly after this to find the angel in tears, her boyfriend in tears and the staff running around trying to comfort them. I was quickly advised by one of the team that the couple had split up.

The angel was being held crying by one of our male office staff. I wanted to run to her, to comfort her, to know what had happened, but I had to allow the events to unfold in their own way. Standing back I watched her sobbing into his shirt.

She later explained to me the events leading up to this parting.

The angel had entered into a discussion with her partner about their relationship, seeking an open discussion of what state it was in, and what they both felt the future held for them. At one stage they had intended marriage and a family. It had just never taken place. They both loved each other and had travelled a long way through life's minefields together. Her partner, our gardener, landed his own bombshell. He said that he had recently realised that he loved her, but was no longer in love with her.

It had become the same for both of them. Theirs had become a relationship of convenience, like so many, rather than one of deep, all-embracing love.

Both had agreed that the end of the journey as lovers had come. They had decided to part, staying like brother and sister, protective and caring of each other.

As the days passed the angel and I started to feel each others presence more and more. Unspoken words of love amassed within our minds, bursting for the opportunity to explode into conversation with each other, expressing our deepest feelings. I had seen her secretly and we had spent time over a meal talking of the future. We were hopelessly in love. I told her that I could no longer conceal my feelings for her. People at work were noticing the energy between us. The words of advice from members of staff to the angel were being given without being sought.

Keep away from him. No good can come of it. He is still married. He is too old for you and you are so different. All of it was starting to get us both down. Something had to change.

Without telling her of my intention I decided to get this out in the open. We had both talked about being open and honest about how we felt for each other. We were just scared about when it would be o.k. to be open. I could wait no longer. I needed to clear the way.

I called her now ex-partner, (our clinic gardener), and my wife from whom I had now been separated for some time. With divorce on the horizon I felt it only appropriate that these two people should know of what the angels and my intent was toward each other. Both agreed to see me without knowing the reason for my visit.

I had become a close friend with her ex partner, and I felt uneasy withholding the knowledge of my love for the angel and my intent towards her. I owed him and my estranged wife the decency of my honesty.

The day of confronting each of them came, and full of nerves I went to see my wife. I sat and told her of me seeing someone else, that I had fallen in love with another woman. Out of respect for her and the marriage that we had both been in for nine years I wanted her to be the first to know.

She repeatedly pushed me to tell her who it was, guessing at people that she thought it might be, I felt unable to tell her before I had broken the news to my new love's ex-partner.

Angry and despondent she told me to leave.

Without taking a breath I drove to see my angel's ex-partner. I was very nervous of him. He was a powerful man, and I was not sure of how he would react. Anticipating a punch or two, I swallowed hard, and knocked on his door.

As he opened the door I was greeted with a big smile and a brotherly hug. My mind raced as I felt that this greeting would soon change when he became aware of the purpose of my visit. Sitting in his one chair in the single room he was now living in, while he sat on the bed, amused by my visit, I felt the sweat running down my back. With eyes twitching and hands trembling I stumbled through explaining the reason for my visit telling him of my love for his ex. All the time I spoke, he never looked up once. He sat fumbling with something he was making, not showing any signs by which I could gauge my next move.

Should I run or should I stay?

As I came to an end of my poorly prepared speech now completely exposed, I awaited his response.

I sat silently, barely breathing, prepared for whatever was to come.

After what seemed like a lifetime of silence he spoke. His face was sullen and not showing any signs of what he felt. He said that in previous years he had been somewhat less controlled with his emotions, and had he still been of that mind now learning of this news, he may have reached under the bed for the claw hammer he kept there and used it to reshape my cranium.

Luckily for both of us he had changed. He gave me a wry smile and said how pleased he was at the news. He had felt that something like this might happen, and for him it was wonderful that this woman he had loved for a long time had found what she deserved in me. He stood and hugged me, then promptly picked up his mobile phone to wish his ex-partner, my angel, his best wishes and love.

She was shocked, unaware that I was there and of what I had done, but relieved. We no longer had to delay or hide the burning love and passion that we held for each other. My relief was complete. As I had started to let go of what was my life and trust that God would fill it with what was right for me, so God did!

We fell into the deepest pool of love that each of us had ever experienced, completely in the open for the whole world to see.

Thank you God!

This is just the beginning. Now leave everything and follow me!

Those words again. What do you mean? I have left my wife and family, I have given over to my ex-wife the family home to live in and a business to support her. What else should I now leave?

Chapter 8

Materialism

By now I had moved in to a small house next door to my friend, The Good Doctor and his partner; I was free to see the angel and was happier than I had ever been. What was I to leave now?

I had left my home, my family and one of my businesses. What else?

Your Life!

Short of dying, which I hope I don't have to do in order to fulfil this guidance, what life?

All that you were!

This left me thinking hard. I remembered once when I was still with my ex- wife, I had been wishing and asking God to relive me of the life I was living. I no longer wished to wear suits and ties, carry a briefcase and be the businessman. Perhaps this is what God meant.

I had toyed with the idea of joining a Tibetan Buddhist monastery, of spending my life in comfortable orange robes learning the meaning of life, caring nothing for the material life that I was trapped in.

Is this what I am meant to do now?

You are on the right track, but your journey is not to be as a Buddhist Monk. You have already had that experience in a past life. Let go of the material things that created the image of who you were!

I think I have got you.

I told my angel of this new guidance. She was not surprised but reaffirmed the importance of letting go of the energy that was held in all of the material items that had made up me, the person that I so longed to be rid of.

The following morning I started to pack all my belongings into black sacks ready to take to the charity shop.

Most of it was easy. Six new suits, countless shirts and ties, shoes, jewellery, and many things that were gifts from the past. I faltered around letting go of certain items like my prised Texan cowboy boots that I had paid $500.00 for and only worn twice.

Whenever I hesitated or faltered in letting something go I heard God say

Living with God

Let go of everything

Everything?

All that you own! Everything that has been you in the material world, which has held you in the experience that you wish to change!

Wow this is tough!

I let go of everything from music to underwear, all that I was wrapped up in. Those clothes and personal effects which I now call my previous life were packed into black bags ready to go.

The next day, dressed in new casual cotton trousers and a shirt that I had bought to wear, a pair of soft shoes and nothing else, I packed all the bags into my car and drove to the local charity shop. As I entered the Red-Cross charity shop I was greeted by two elderly ladies dressed in tweed skirts and flat brown leather shoes, like clones of each other made specifically to work in charity shops, both of them skilfully adept at dealing with all kinds of sadness that life brought to their door. I asked if they would like the items packed in my car. (happily) they responded positively and took the sacks from me as I unloaded what had been my life onto the shop floor. I looked at it lying there. How pathetic it now seemed. I had spent my life holding on to these things in order to make myself feel safe and important.

Raven

There I was dead on the shop floor.

The staff looked at me with great concern on their faces and asked who had died.

"I have", I replied with a huge grin on my face.

A bemused look came over the faces of those ladies. I am sure they thought I was some sort of crackpot.

As I left the shop an image came to me of someone finding my Texan cowboy boots and thinking what luck they had had finding them.

The truth was, what luck I was having losing them.

I walked away feeling even more free than I was before, elated from this experience.

I was ready to start my new life without these crutches.

I was experiencing freedom from the material world I had grown up in.

This feeling became a new drug to me. I felt as though I had been reborn and I was grateful. I spent more time in quiet meditation, something I had played at in the past never being able to achieve the bliss that others spoke of.

It was happening now for me. The more I did it the more powerful it became.

The conversations and teachings I was receiving were becoming more and more detailed.

Chapter 9

Canada

In the month of June 2004 my new partner and I were invited to attend a spiritual journey to Canada. A group of about sixteen people including my friend, the Good Doctor his partner and two other members of our clinic staff were going.

My partner was keen to go and quite honestly such was the bliss I was enjoying within our relationship. There was no way that I was going to be away from her for two weeks. I readily booked to go. The trip was to Lake Louise in Banff national park one of the most beautiful places on Earth. Lake Louise contains the vortex of Archangel Michael, an energy that some of these people had been working with. I did not know what all this meant, but I was intrigued.

The attitudes within the clinic were becoming more biased towards the spiritual element of life. It was becoming obvious that we would have to close down the clinical practice of treating terminal cancer patients because of pressure from powerful people that did not like us creating something that worked and they did not control. So for me this would be a good insight into the world of spiritualism. This was a world of which I knew very little outside of my own personal experiences. I hoped that with this group I might find common ground with other people who might not consider what I had been experiencing as totally crazy. They might be able to shed more light on who or what I was hearing.

Throughout my life I had a history of defying systems and normal things. If someone said, "You can't do that", I did it anyway, a childish way of retaliating to what I had been told as a child that I would never achieve anything. I know it was childish, but it had created some interesting results in my life. Where others had failed, I succeeded. Where others succeeded I normally failed. It seemed to give me some sort of excitement to be able to do what others had failed at. I had spent some time in the British army and they had found my attitude towards life useful at times. I was the type of person that cared nothing for myself and so was perfect for the type of jobs that others declined.

I had spent a lifetime of struggle, fighting to keep things alive against all the odds. Statements like "going with the flow" were not in my vocabulary. I never really took the time to think what that statement meant or any of the often used clichés in life.

Words were a source of simple communication to me, a system for getting what I wanted done, and so here I was going on a spiritual journey, something I would never have done before.

Living with God

Now God had brought about a way that I would immerse myself into whatever he had planned for my spiritual growth in Canada. I was following this angel that I had fallen in love with. It could have been down a coal mine for all I cared. God knew that I would follow her anywhere, and God wanted me there to begin a journey into deeper spiritual awareness.

Quite honestly I would have joined The Moonies if it meant staying close to her. Whatever The Moonies are, I mean no disrespect in saying that.

I was caught in a flow deeply swallowed up in the love that I was experiencing that was taking me somewhere that I neither cared about nor thought of as long as I was with my angel. For once I had let go of all control of any outcome in my life.

Love was carrying me where it wanted to take me.

On arrival in Canada we met with some American friends who we had worked with before. One of them was the man that I had met earlier who had channelled my dead daughter Emma to me. Everyone was excited at the thought of two weeks in this beautiful country and a little excited at what was to happen. I was totally excited at the thought of spending this time with the angel.

Many things did happen on that journey. We visited waterfalls and caves, mountains and lakes more stunning than I can ever explain. The country and the energy I felt there took my breath away. For me one of the most significant things was to happen at the end of our trip, just before we left to come home.

Raven

For most of the journey we stayed together as a group, sharing everything from our food to our experiences, some of them very emotional.

I learned that I had found a group that were as sensitive as I was. I felt safe and able to be totally open with them. After ten days all the group work had finished, and people were going home at different times, some to Texas, some to California, New York and so on. We were staying for three extra days, and we had arranged a private channelling in our room with one of the journey leaders, a man who I had become quite attached to, called Maitreya, a tall man with a very gentle energy. I felt a kindred spirit with him. He was a wise man who had shared with me some of the traumatic episodes of his life originally born in Canada, but now living in New York. This had been a very special journey for him coming back to his birthplace.

Maitreya channelled the energy to us known as Black Hawk. This was the energy of an American Indian who sat and talked with us for two hours.

It was at this meeting that something changed for me. I had asked why all of this change had happened for me. Why had I met and fallen in love with this angel? Why was my life changing so much from what it had been in the past?

The answer was simple. I had come into alignment with Spirit.

I had stopped working against God and had accepted that following God would be a better path for me to take.

I was not totally aware of what all this meant, but it turned out to be one of the most significant conversations of my life so far.

Living with God

In this conversation we were also told to visit a shaman, a holy man who was skilled in the ancient practice of shamanism, to have our energy cleared of the past. Luckily I had met a shaman on a workshop that I had been involved in some years previously. The workshop was on a subject called "Remote Viewing" given by a very interesting American called David Moorhouse. (That is another story on its own).

This course was filled with about twenty other people from all walks of life including scientists, air force pilots, the head of the United Kingdom, U.F.O. organisation, homeopaths and ordinary people who were just interested like me.

Sitting next to me on this three day course was a man called Leo. He looked like Father Christmas with his long white beard. Over the days of the course we had become quite friendly, and I had learned from him of his life as a shaman. This was the man we would seek out on our return to England to carry out the advice given by Black Hawk.

In the time that we spent in Canada we became closer to all of the people within the group, sharing some quite extraordinary experiences, and more importantly to me, I became much more aware of whom the people were that I had been working with in the clinic. I also realised that in meeting these people I was no longer alone in this world. There are so many people like me who have had similar experiences which science and much of mainstream society just cannot explain.

I knew then that I was not going mad just becoming more aware of the world I live in and just how little I knew about it, I became aware of energy as a powerful force that has enormous impact on us human beings. From the energy given off by one human to another to the energy created by mass mental thought, to the energy created by spiritual forces beyond our scope of comprehension.

In those last three days of our time in Canada the Angel and I spent our time alone walking the rivers and snow capped mountainsides of this incredible place, oblivious of everything around us, completely lost in the love we were feeling together.

Sadly it all had to end, those three days of bliss fading away into the all too present hassle of travelling.

Chapter 10

The end of one creation and the beginning of another

Back in England after a long flight from Canada we were greeted on the first Monday after coming back by two men from the medicines control agency. These men had arrived at the clinic unannounced to carry out an inspection. The clinic was fondly called "Tannery House", a name that was given to our old Georgian building as it was linked to the origins of the local industry. The house had belonged to the owner of the local tannery which was once the main employer of the small village we were in.

The two men from the medicines control agency were like heavies from the Mafia. Dressed in dark suits and with menacing expressions they advised us that they had been to the local pharmacy directly across the road from the clinic and advised the pharmacist that they should no longer accept medical prescriptions written from the two doctors

Raven

in our practice. Without discussion we were closed down forthwith.

Whoever or whatever did not want us to succeed was using powers that we were unable to combat. We realised that we lived in a world that certainly did not allow freedom of choice. The medicines control agency had the right to tell everyone what was best for them and could do whatever they wished without any avenue of recourse open to us that would allow our small business to stay alive.

Such was their power.

Was this fate, destiny or just a corrupt system denying the freedom of choice to the sick and dying? Who knows?

To all of us it was the end of what we had all worked so hard to create. To the many hundreds of people who were literally dying and desperate to come to our centre it was all over.

It took time for the shock of what had just happened to set in. All of us walked around in the centre for several days stunned. The staff were all twitchy looking to The Good Doctor, his partner and myself for inspiration. We had nothing to offer them. The three of us finally agreed that we had to take some action. These people were still on our payroll. I set about telling all of the staff of our misfortune in detail and started the process of laying them off telling them all to seek new employment thanking them all for the commitment they had given to the centre and the people who had come there for healing.

This was a sad occasion for all of us. It was one of the hardest things I had ever done. All of these people had found a home that they were happy in. The centre had

Living with God

given these doctors and nurses a new sense of purpose and achievement. They had come from a system that provided no job satisfaction, where patients were numbers in beds, where people suffered at the hands of uncaring bureaucrats who were interested in money rather than the dignity of human life.

I felt sorry for all of them. They had considered that they had found a job for life, working in a new system that filled the gap that the government health service left gaping open, like a wound that was not healing but getting worse. For the first time in their careers they had found the way to heal that wound, and now it was over.

Medical and office staff alike were all angry. Slowly, one by one, accepting the situation they left.

The centre was dismantled piece by piece medical machinery, computers and furniture. I walked around the building often, watching it being stripped. This building which had once been full of hope and activity was now empty nothing but a shell. Only the memory of the past lingered in the walls. I could stand in a room and see all that had happened there and in a flash all gone again. Only the silence remained hanging in the air. It felt like the life had been squeezed out of it. Now it stood waiting for the next adventure that would befall this great house.

The angel and I were alone. With nothing more to do we decided that it would be wise to continue with the guidance we had received in Canada and went to see Leo the shaman.

We met Leo at his home in the gentle hills of Kent. To everyone outside it was a normal detached country house nestling on a quiet country lane. When we entered the building it transformed into museum of American Indian artefacts. There were hundreds of bands of Indians in each tribe and hundreds of tribes all over America, and pretty much all of those tribes had some form of representation in the house in the form of pictures or drums or ceremonial wands. Leo was such a quiet man, proud of his collection each of which carried a story that he was happy to tell us of. What a fascinating man.

In the garden to the side and rear of the house Leo had built sweat lodges for cleansing and pits dug into the earth for practicing rituals of live burial (staying underground overnight to become connected with the earth). A full size medicine wheel was laid out at the end of his garden. Close to it was another large circle of stones and inside this circle there were logs for people to sit on which all centred on a fire used to purify the spirit and ward off negative energies. We were taken through an ancient American Indian ceremony of energy clearance, freeing us of the past and all of its hooks.

It was at this ceremony that I had one of the strangest experiences.

While sitting alone in the medicine wheel after Leo had finished working with me and had left me to reflect on the ceremony, I heard a voice say to me,

---

Are you now ready to work with me?

Living with God

Thinking that this was just another rambling of my mind I ignored it and carried on taking in my experience with Leo. It came again:

"Are you now ready to work with me?"

Intrigued at what was happening I decided to answer the voice to see what this was all about and where it went!
 "Who are you?"

Jesua!

Am I going nuts? Do you mean Jesus?

Jesua, Yahweh, Jesus, Sananda, The Christ Light. I am all one and the same!

Are you the voice that I have been calling God?

One and the same!

I am going nuts? Perhaps all of this has just tipped me over the edge into insanity.

No! You have just come to a place where, should you choose to, we can work together!

Should I choose to? What does that mean?

It means working with me for seven years, communicating the word of God. You are one of our chosen communicators!

A little shocked and yet amused I sat and pondered what was happening. What did I have to lose? My entire world had already changed, and I was at a loss as to what I was going to do next anyway.

Does this mean channelling like some of the people I have been working with?

If you wish to call it that!

I accept!

Are you sure?

I think so, I said feeling quite nervous and completely mad.

What do I have to do?

I was thinking that the next thing I would have to do would be to sit cross legged in front of hoards of people seeking spiritual enlightenment, while being dressed in flowing robes and becoming some sort of guru. My ego loved the idea of this!

Living with God

> *This means first of all entering IN-TUITION!*

I am a little confused. Isn't intuition following my instincts?

> *No, it is becoming teachable; you are ready to be In-Tuition, ready to be taught the ways of God! Before you can communicate, you must first learn what it is that you are to communicate. You are ready for IN-TUITION!*

I did not feel so happy at about this; in-tuition meant me having to learn something which meant work. Hmmm! I had spent all my life thinking that I knew best and that I knew all I needed to know. My ego had become so inflated. I had become fed up with learning and wanted to do some living.

> *What you have learned so far has got you where you are! In pain! Lost! Confused!*

Wow are you listening to my thoughts? That's unfair. I have been following the guidance, letting go of my family, my home, my business, my clothes. Am I not ready now?

> *You have cleared some of the debris of your past. You are now ready for IN-TUITION.*

Raven

But I have met and fallen in love with the angel. My life has become free and better. I have been working with spiritual people. I have started to accept God in my life. This is the best my life has ever been. Isn't it this way because I have evolved spiritually? Isn't it because I am now spiritual?

No! It is this way because you have finally decided to follow the path of God instead of your own. Meeting the angel and falling in love are just the beginning. As you let go of what was your past God fills it with the new. What you have experienced in this new love and freedom is just the beginning. Let's call it a little taste of the divine! Follow me and you will start to know the divine and all its glory. Experience the power of God, the Love of God and know what it is to serve others rather than yourself.

In serving others through your in-tuition you will truly come to know peace, freedom, love and abundance beyond your comprehension. In learning to live with God you will enter the kingdom of heaven while on Earth, living in God's house.

I'm sold. Where do I sign? I have always been attracted to having more and living better.

Then so it is!

Ok. What do I do now?

All in good time, your lessons have already begun! Go about your business and we will talk again soon.

I was excited. I had to sit and wait patiently for the Angel to finish her ceremony with Leo before I could tell her of my experience. My mind was running riot with the words that had been spoken to me, running ahead creating all sorts of fantasies that I was really enjoying, but still there was that doubt hanging in the back of my mind, you are nuts, you have finally flipped, ready for the straitjacket.

I was to learn later that this inner doubt was one of the worst demons that I would battle with over and over again. It would be the little sneak in the night when all I was left with was the silence of myself, creeping into my conscious mind telling me this is all horseshit. You know better than this crap. Follow me. I can get you out of all this. Have faith in yourself not all this bollocks! My faith in what I was hearing would be tested to the max.

The day with Leo came to its end. We had been cleared energetically of all the past. We both felt another level of freedom and peace from the ceremonies we had undergone, and we had had our relationship blessed by all the spirits of the American Indian world.

We felt good and very much in love. What a journey this was turning out to be. I had long wanted to experience this underworld of spirituality, talking with people who lived a life that seemed beyond this mundane physical experience that I had become part of.

My life experience as a child had taught me that more existed than the three dimensional restrictions of this world, and I was starting to really know what it felt like to allow my body and mind the freedom of acceptance that all was not just work, money and more than the Jones's. I was no longer in a suit and tie, governed by the cruel restrictive practices of modern society. I felt as if I was entering an entirely new world. Every day was introducing me to new and exciting happenings.

We thanked Leo for all his work and the amazing time we had spent with him. We were hugged warmly by this figure of total peace and happiness. We felt as though we had made a wonderful new friend of someone who had been just an acquaintance. We got into the car, and before we had left the drive, I was into a verbal explosion to the Angel of my experience in the medicine wheel.

She sat quietly smiling, nodding at all of my enthusiastic explanations, allowing me the complete excitement of telling her what had taken place in the medicine wheel. I was like a small child who had just had its first visit to the funfair.

To her it was all completely normal. Not surprised at all and yet not detracting from my experience. She allowed me to go on until I was spent of words and enthusiasm.

Living with God

We returned to the clinic mostly in blissful silence, just relating the odd thing that had come back to our memories from the trip. We sat holding hands for the complete journey. I so much love this incredible being, my Angel.

As we pulled into the gate of Tannery House I was brought back to earth with a bump, looking at this empty building. It was so sad to see it bereft of all life.

On entering the building I was aware of an energy that had existed when we were open as a clinic. Then it had felt like a very minor background energy that now seemed to fill every inch of the building and was so prominent it took my breath away. I thought that this was just more obvious since the building had been cleared, and I overlooked the importance of it.

What were we to do with this place now? A large mortgage on the building still had to be paid, running costs like heating, utilities and maintenance...

This building will become a spiritual centre a place of healing that deals with the real issue of disease. You will purchase the building. It will be called The Lighthouse.

What? How can I do that? No money no income, no system of how to create it. This sounds beyond possible. The voice of Sananda boomed the words again in my ears,

---

You will purchase the building!

Raven

How?

Have faith in us. Call back the staff that would wish to remain here healing the sick. Speak to them of what we wish for this place and for them. Allow yourself to accept us. We will work through you. Your actions will be ours, our words will spring from your mouth, and your thoughts will be ours. Have faith and all will be well.

I sat with this guidance for some time. My brain was trying to figure out how all of this could work. My mind was trying to use logic, and there was no logic in what I was hearing. It sounded great, but my brain could not twist itself into understanding the practicalities of how or by what means all this could happen. By any school of business what was to become my intention following the guidance was nothing short of madness!

Seeking out my Angel, I told her of this news and as always she nodded, agreeing at what a great thing this would be, totally accepting that all of this would happen and without a second thought of how. Her faith was so strong that she did not allow her brain to interfere with her serenity by clogging up the system with the inept logical aspects of the human mind that would be translated into physical fear and control, which I was still full of.

At times in my life, when fear was a silent partner in my brain, I had experienced what I now call miracles, things

Living with God

that had happened without any logical reasoning. It was this knowledge that I relied on to carry out this guidance, coupled with my growing faith of what I was hearing. We discussed this with The Good Doctor and his partner. Together they were the overall major shareholders in Tannery House. They had to agree to this illogical proposal. To my great surprise they did so without blinking an eye.

They had come to trust me over a very long friendship. We had achieved things that they had never considered possible. Both of them were living what anyone else would call a spiritual life, and they readily accepted not only the proposal for the ongoing use and purchase of the building, but also they seemed to accept the fact that I was being guided by spirit in the form of Sananda.

We agreed on a number of people that had shown a deeper interest in a spiritual life path who we would invite back to the centre. All of these people had worked with us before, and we knew them reasonably well.

Throughout the life of Tannery House they had shown deep spiritual compassion and caring for the people that had come to us. These would be the people that would help to lead forward this new project.

Together we invited them to meet with us. This caused a great excitement for us and for those who came. All the time the fear was within me like a crouching tiger waiting to pounce in the form of unbridled fear, constantly purring in my ear the words of doubt, attaching itself to any weakness of thought that entered my mind. Time after time it attacked me making me want to give up and run to the hills.

Raven

At the meeting of this new group that would establish this spiritual centre, we sat together on the floor of what had been the main treatment room of Tannery House.

Here cancer patients and their families had sat receiving care and love, hope and guidance. Now we sat together, unlike before as employers and employees, but as equals. Every voice had a right to be heard. All would be leaders of this wonderful new concept.

Some of this group had greater faith than others, but for the moment we were all of the same mind and intent. We started to discuss together the different ways that we could make The Lighthouse work. I sat back and watched with a big smile as the enthusiasm in the room grew. It felt like we were on the right track, an odd group of people that had come together again to use our knowledge to help others.

All the ideas were put together. Nothing was discounted, and different members of the group started to take responsibility for some of the ideas that were being formed. Some weeks passed with the ideas being put into action. We had all agreed that no one would receive pay until The Lighthouse was functioning and self supporting. We had all come together to make this work.

We were contacted by our American friend, the man who had brought my dead daughter back to me in a channelling. He said that he wished to contribute by coming to England to put on a channelling for us and all who wished to attend and that the proceeds should be given towards the upkeep of The Lighthouse. This caused another stir amongst us as what we had been doing so far, although enthusiastically,

Living with God

was doing little to nothing towards raising funds, and the bills were already starting to mount.

Everything that we had put on was to be paid for by voluntary contribution, and the mental and physical enthusiasm shown so far was not being matched with the same financial enthusiasm by those that had come.

This proposal from our American friend rekindled the energy within the group that had already started to crumble. Belief was disappearing fast, but for the moment everyone threw their weight behind this spark of light.

Letters were sent to everyone we knew, telephone calls made, posters placed in appropriate places talking of this event.

When our American friend arrived, he and I spent some time talking together. I told him of what had happened to me and of my agreement to work with Sananda. He was a little taken aback and I watched his mind clicking fast as he took in this news. Later in the day we all sat together as a group and started to talk. I knew inside me the purpose of this meeting although nothing had been said as to why we were getting together right now.

I knew that our American friend wanted to test this new channel that I had become to find out if this was for real or not. As the group sat talking of nothing specific, I felt the energy of Sananda building within me like a small flame to begin with. As it grew, the fear within me grew faster. I did not wish to channel in front of this man. He had been my teacher, the one I had sought for advice, the leader on several spiritual journeys that I had attended; he was the one that had spent a lifetime on his spiritual journey taking over from his mother as a channel. As I sat within the circle as a part of the group, I noticed my American friend glancing at me often from the corner of his eye, silently urging this spiritual communication. I had had many reasons to be scared in my life, but the fear I felt right in this moment matched the worst of them.

The flame grew into a furnace within me, Sananda was going to speak, and I felt that my chest would burst as I tried to hold back this raging fire over which I was quickly loosing any control. Would this all turn out to be a sham, to be cast down in front of my peers like a common trickster who had lured these good people into a web of control and manipulation?

I felt I wanted to get up and run, make some excuse to leave the room before anything happened.

As I tried to raise myself from the floor, I felt myself become completely helpless. My body no longer responded to my mental commands; I was rooted to the floor unable to move.

As quickly as I realised this my mind sank into complete peace. I was now entirely out of control. I had left the building that was my body; someone or something else was in charge.

Blessings my beloved. Welcome!

The room became silent and all eyes turned towards my body. I was seeing everything, aware of everything, and yet in control of nothing including my own body.

Living with God

The silence was deafening. All eyes were glued to this body that the voice had come from, my body, and I sat like a visitor within myself waiting for whatever was to happen next. My American friend's voice boomed,

"In the name of Christ's love and light are you of the light?"

I am the light!

Again, "In the name of Christ's love and light are you of the light?"

I am the light!

For the third time he said again, In the name of Christ's love and light are you of the light?"

I am the light, the light that shines in all mankind. Welcome!

The eyes of my body and those of my American friend remained locked in a silent battle, the battle that goes on in all mankind when confronted with things beyond the three dimensional world of reality that we lock ourselves into. A battle going on inside me, the battle was not accepting or acceptance of what was happening. Could this be true or not? We were both in it for that elongated moment before relaxing into this ethereal communication.

Raven

Your wife is to have another child, and that child will be a boy! We will rejoice the coming of this new spirit.

The American sat silent and stunned for a moment choosing to let this statement fly from the room as though the wind had collected it as quickly as it was spoken and then removed it from existence. This was not about his family or anything other than a challenge of the validity of who was present, Sananda or a hoax. The American spoke again. If this is the house of God why do you allow such things as this to be openly displayed in the corridors for all to observe?"

He stood and walked powerfully out of the room, returning a few moments later clutching a picture frame which contained a vow of abundance.

The Lighthouse was filled with these hanging on many of the walls. They were public statements of visitors who had come to The Lighthouse. They stated their own acceptance of abundance in their life, that they were now ready to receive all that God had to offer them.

They contained the word DESIRE several times.

It was this word that my friend was pointing to vigorously; saying that all of his spiritual teachers from Sai Baba to Red Feather had taught him that desire was the root of all evil, and therefore this thing should not be acceptable here in God's house.

How can life exist in human form without desire? Desire is as necessary to life as oxygen. Without it how could the human form move from one level of experience to another, ever evolving, ever growing satisfying man's desire to learn and his thirst for knowledge? Man's innate desire is to better himself and create a better world for his family. Without desire how could man love woman and vice versa? Nothing can or does exist without first being created from a desire, the desire to eat, sleep, procreate. To consider the meaning of the word desire and even worse personally having a desire as evil, or knowing the word as the root of all evil is misunderstanding the meaning given to it by the teachers who said it.

In the context in which it is put within this vow of abundance, which is a desire for the wealth of God's design for God's abundance, it is accepting openly to oneself and to all who wish to read it, as well as God, that the person making the vow is now ready to receive all that has always been available to man. God has always wished for you, and all, more than mankind has ever wished for himself. Moreover it has always

Raven

been available. Without your desire, the love you seek will evade you! It is only man himself who has stopped himself from receiving God's abundance. He has not allowed himself the desire.

I was more stunned than anyone else at this response. The room fell into silence again. The American took his seat and his steely black eyes locked again with the eyes of my body. A smile came across my face. It was not mine; I was still trying to run away. The smile was not returned for some time as the American fought with himself to accept what he had heard. Finally he relaxed into himself, allowing his body to give up the fight. He accepted who and what he had been talking to. Relief hit him and he smiled "saying" I was told that I would have a girl."

It will be a boy!

After a few more minor communications the end of the channelling came with the American moving over to my body and thanking sincerely through his words and eyes the presence within me Sananda.

    A relief came over the whole room; a smile was entering the eyes and mouths of all present As chatter started to enter the room I felt the energy of Sananda fading from my body. I felt elated and weary at the same time. That had been an ordeal. My American friend hugged me and thanked me for an amazing experience. My teachers changed that day.

I became a hungry student of Sananda. My American friend would always be one of my teachers and still is to this day, but my daily education now came from this new source.

The group in the room started to break up. Some of them had had their confidence rekindled in what was working through me for the time being.

(Over a year later my American friend and his wife had a new arrival. It was a boy).

The following days were filled with more preparations for the forthcoming Saturday, the big day when our American friend would channel to the collective group that we were all hoping would be large.

On the Saturday morning my American friend asked me if I would join him in the main room to prepare it for the coming event. I agreed and did so while other members of our group made sure that everything else was ready. My friend and I spent several hours cleansing the room with sage as used by the American Indians. We played Asian Indian music in the room invoking all of the spirits that would join us for the big day. The floor was scattered with rose petals. Candles burned in every space that would not be taken up by a visitor. Crystals of every kind were scattered around the room. It felt very special.

We had both dressed for the occasion and then sat in quiet meditation waiting for all the guests to arrive. At around 2.00 pm it started. People flooded into the centre, people of all kinds, people I had never seen before and some who I had. Men, women, children, young and old, people from all walks of life. We sat in silence as the room filled. More chairs were brought in. Furniture moved to make space until we

Raven

could take no more. Standing space had been filled. Young people had given up chairs for the elderly. The doorway was filled with people standing, craning to get sight and sound of what was to happen.

A silence came over the room and my American friend broke into channelling an energy we had all come to know and love as Red Feather. Red Feather spoke for a considerable time to the people in the room collectively and sometimes personally. I realised for the first time in my life how much hunger existed in society for connection with something beyond the human.

Every person there was glued to what was being said. Often tears flowed from different people as they were given information that was particular to them. Jaws of some hung open that had never witnessed such an event. As I sat I became aware of the energy Sananda growing in me as it had every time I was about to enter channel. Again the fear rose in me. I did not want to do this. Up until now I had only channelled to people who were aware of what I was doing and had some belief. Here I was presented with members of the public that had never seen anything like this. I fought to stop this energy growing in me.

This is not about you. Get out of the way and allow your ego to subside, for it is your ego that tries to control this communication through your fear of people's judgement of you. You are the channel through which we communicate. You are not the message.

Living with God

I felt told! As small and insignificant as I had ever felt. My ego had been controlling me and my actions for so long. I started to relax, feeling the Angel sitting close beside me. The warmth of her body soothed me. The unconditional love that I was wrapped in given by her without conscious knowledge held me. The energy within me grew and I gave way to it.

Look to each other with love and kindness, not judgements manipulations and control, jealousy, hatred and fear. Are you truly giving of yourself? Love each other and allow each other to enjoy the gifts of God Spend time in nature feeling the love of God.

The gentleness of the wind in your face, the coolness of the grass under your feet, the beauty of the flowers that bloom for your pleasure, the warmth of the sun on your back. Every moment of your life is filled with opportunity, not struggle. It is your choices and your perspective that determines the outcome of your decision. All of you are in search of God! And yet you fail to see, looking beyond yourself for something that has and always will exist within you. Look not to others to make your life complete, happy or fulfilled. Look to yourself to answer the pains that you wish God to heal. The answers to them all, the cure to all ills, lies within being. In accepting that God lives within you so will you learn to live with God, being as God is.

I have struggled to write that as much as I struggled with my body being used for it to be said on the day; my ego, fear and judgement is still with me.

My moment of channelling came to its end for this event. Red Feather took over again taking questions and finally bringing the event to a close some three to four hours later. As people filed past Red Feather each collected the gift of a crystal as they left.

The Angel and I sat in silence. One of the messages that had been given by Red Feather was that this new Lighthouse would be governed by a council of eight people, and that any people considering themselves to be one of those eight should wait until all others had left.

As people left the building a bowl had been placed by the door for those who chose to give a donation for what they had received, which would be used for the ongoing upkeep of the centre.

The door closed as the last person left.

Eleven people remained in the room including my American friend, the Angel and myself.

We all looked at each other aware that we counted 11, a greater number than was required for the task of running the Lighthouse.

Eyes were darting from one to another looking to see if that person or this person would be the one told to leave.

Our American friend was not going to be one of the eight which left two more that had to go.

My friend spoke," Who is here that, will not be a member of this council?"

I stood and said that although I had been given the guidance to purchase this building for spirit I knew that my role was not to stay here after. My role was to travel and continue the work that I had undertaken with Sananda. I thanked them all and left the room. I walked up the stairs to my old office which now lay empty and I sat on the floor wondering what was to happen to my Angel and myself. Would she stay and be a part of this centre, or would she also leave and come and join me?

Two minutes later the Angel left the room and came to me hugging me and saying that our place was together enjoying the gift of love that we had been granted. I was so happy about her decision; all I could focus on was how much I loved her.

The meeting in the main room ended some 30 minutes later, and the group came out to join the Angel and me in the dining area, where a buffet had been prepared for all that wished to partake. We all talked and basked in what had been a very enjoyable day. Some minutes later my American friend entered the dining room and strode up to me. He advised me that not enough money had even been raised to cover his airfare, so there was nothing left for the centre.

He told me that the council of eight was now advised of what it was to do. This council was made up of The Good Doctor and his partner, other members of our previous staff and some outsiders who had attended on the day. He told me that my ongoing task was to secure the finance for the purchase of the building and then to produce a salary system for these eight people.

I was a little daunted at this thought, considering that not a penny had come in from the day's event.

How was I going to raise a million pounds for the purchase of this building and provide a salary for eight people, create an income sufficient to support the mortgage, enough income for the ongoing upkeep of the building and all the bills? All with no definable income stream. I decided to allow it all to happen by whatever scheme God had up his sleeve, my head just couldn't cope with the dilemma. I enjoyed the rest of the day allowing this task to fall deeply to the back of my mind.

I had now moved into the small cottage in the grounds of the centre with my Angel. After everyone had left we locked the main building and returned to the small but cosy comfort of our own space. The love I was experiencing with her made everything else that I would have worried myself sick about in the past insignificant. I had learned from my daughter's death how insignificant these matters were. Love was all and still is all that matters.

We sat together closely on the settee and the thought came to my mind, I had never been as happy as I was now.

Even with all the money in the world and all the materialism in the world. Give me love over and above it. I know its true value.

Unbeknown to me just how much I valued love was going to be tested later.

After this weekend the Angel and I left for a break from all of the commotion, leaving The Good Doctor and the council to begin their tasks. The Angel and I spent the next weeks together solely exploring the depths of our new found love, talking and playing. For both of us this was an adventure into the unknown. Neither of us had known love like this before. Previously life had been planned. All that we ever did had had a known outcome. This was pleasure beyond belief. Before we had left for our break I had received a message from spirit.

Experience love without the male physical release for yourself!

What?

You are joking after what I have just been through. I am about to go away with this goddess to experience love, peace and pleasure and you are telling me we can't.

This had been the first holiday that either of us had been on for many years. Please tell me you are joking.

We are not joking and we never said both of you. We just said you are to refrain from the male physical release for 14 days.

I felt the anger rise in me, and I protested heavily unable to believe what I was hearing.

We were in love and I wanted to express it.

The Angel looked at me smiling as I was recanting this message,. This part of our journey was for her to know the wonder of physical love experienced with the entire focus upon her only.

She was happy. I was angry and amused at the same time. As my anger abated, which did take a little while, I settled into the prospect of being with this goddess, focusing on her pleasure only. Eventually the thought of this created an excitement in me of a kind I had never felt before.

Over the next 14 days I felt the real male in me rise like a howling furnace; I felt a power that was like I had been injected with energy and passion from a thousand men. My maleness was raging from my body straining at the seams, unable to burst its torrent of love, which served the purpose of increasing the pleasure experienced by my Angel.

For the next 14 days I loved this woman like never before. I became aware of her needs, her desires, her pleasures, and the more I loved her, the more pleasure I received from her experience. We fell more and more in love. The message I had received before leaving England for this holiday, had been one of the most powerful messages I have ever had to date. I was learning the beauty and power, the ecstasy of love experienced by giving to another solely.

Throughout this time of her pleasure I was being guided on how to please this goddess that I was with, my Angel. I was being visited by a female spirit. This spirit guided my hands, my body, my mouth and even my breath. The Angel and I were feeling pleasures that were not of this earth. Orgasm after orgasm, mental and physical, poured through the Angel's body like a never ending river of sheer ecstasy. She was learning to accept for the first time in her life the joy of being loved.

Everything focussed entirely on her and her pleasure.

God had taught me another valuable lesson, the value of giving to someone else in this way. I found pleasure beyond anything I had ever encountered before by giving of myself unconditionally to someone else without thought of my own release.

The stereotypical male mould had been well and truly smashed for the Angel. Both of us found a new freedom. I am not sure who the female voice belonged to who visited me as I loved the Angel, guiding my every movement. What I do know is that she taught me invaluable lessons that this man will never forget.

We returned to England after our break floating on a cloud of sheer pleasure and love. That has stayed with us ever since. At The Lighthouse we met with the council and talked briefly of what had happened in our absence. The answer was brief. Nothing! Nothing was happening. They had found dead ends to all their endeavours to create a flow of work and support from outside visitors.

They all looked to me. My brain switched into the old fashioned process of business plans and financial proposals that would be considered by the traditional money lending houses to refinance the property. I set about preparing them and told the council what I was doing, and that they were to meet with Sananda daily to continue the work that had been started by our American friend.

I started to contact some of my old colleagues from my business days to get some help sourcing the financial package that was needed. All I found was silence; no one wanted to know. After many days of searching one of my contacts came up with a financial source prepared to help. I was given an offer of £980,000 on bridging finance which meant an interest rate of 17% over a six month period. This was legal extortion, but the advisor told me it was the only way to do what I wanted. After six months we would be able to switch the loan to a normal high street lender at the standard rates for the time which were around 6%.

With my heart in my mouth I accepted the offer subject to valuation. By this time our company Tannery House Ltd. Had been voluntarily put into liquidation, and the receiver handling the affair was becoming a little twitchy because the property had not yet been sold. As it was the main asset in the business it needed to be sold to wind up the company and clear the debt to the bank.

By now the situation was getting difficult with the winding up procedure of our previous business. As some months had passed an official receiver had been appointed, and she wanted to see some action. A meeting was called by her and I went to this meeting with the two owners of Tannery House Ltd. The Good Doctor and his partner, who were also feeling very nervous about the situation. Our relationship had started to deteriorate, and in the opinion of The Good Doctor God was not delivering what had been promised, and his belief in God and me understandably was waning fast.

At this meeting no one was aware of the deal I had negotiated with the finance house, and as I entered the room where this official meeting was taking place, the receiver and my two partners were sitting solemn faced fully expecting to have a discussion on selling the property on the open market and ending the prospect of the building being transferred to The Lighthouse and the care of the council of eight, two of which were The Good Doctor and his partner.

The meeting started and quickly moved to the issue of the property; by this time The Good Doctor and his partner were agitated with me and The Lighthouse project. They quickly agreed and passed a motion to sell the property as fast as possible to the first interested party via a property auction. A very sound idea as we all had personal money invested in the Georgian building and would like to get it back.

I pulled from my pocket the letter of offer from the finance house and handed them each a copy.

Silence!

As they all read the details, not interested in the financial cost of this package, they all accepted the deal and my offer to purchase the property at the given loan value £980,000.00 minus purchase costs. The meeting quickly ended and we all left. It appeared that everyone was happy with this arrangement, even though I could feel that The Good Doctor did not trust me any longer. On my return to the Angel I advised her of the outcome of the meeting and proceeded to instruct a qualified property surveyor to asses the value of the building and land as needed by the finance house in order proceed with the loan.

The days passed and the council, the Angel and I met regularly with spirit in the energy form of Sananda.

We thank you for your commitment. As we move forward together it is time to look within yourselves. Consider your motive for being here. Ask yourself, "Am I being as good as I can be?" To teach means first to be Being is the way that others will learn from you. In order to live with God you must first learn how to live with God.

This means cleaning house. You all know what lies within yourself, anger, jealousy, opinions, manipulation, control, lies, deceit, love of materialism and money, fear. This is just the beginning Now is the time to leave them all behind, to become free of all these things and more. These character defects are the crosses that man carries. For all of you a new freedom lies ahead, to be free of these things to love all unconditionally, to learn to give of yourself without thought of reward. You will learn to look to your fellows with kindness. To live with God as all of you indicated you do means to set yourself free of them.

This was the message that we all heard. The message was a ticking bomb. For many, being spiritual meant talking of angels and of things beyond physical reach, of the stars and celestial beings, of planets aligning and a new world all very heady and intangible. The last thing some of those people wanted to hear was the need to start looking at their own actions. Some of them certainly were not spiritual.

Looking at how we were all living our lives, as long as it did not mean them changing, everyone was in for the journey. This message changed everything. I looked around the room at the contorted faces. Anger and embarrassment were heavy objects of energy that hung in the air like buzzards waiting to pick the flesh from our bones. This was not what everyone wanted to hear. Everyone had come to help the sick and needy, to wrap them up in unearthly claptrap that only served ego.

It was not long before things started to change. Sananda started to help individuals to see themselves warts and all, the things that needed to change before we could even consider helping others. As Sananda taught us the group got smaller and smaller. Excuses from people as to why they could not come that day started to arrive with staggering frequency, and those who sent them disappeared from all communication.

Within a matter of six weeks all were gone but for three.

The Angel, Patrick (my Angels ex partner) and I!

We were now at a stage when income for all of us was becoming critical; food was becoming scarcer as we sat daily learning from Sananda. The three of us were changing significantly as we openly offered ourselves to be stripped naked of our defects by God in front of each other. Nothing was left out; all of our personal character faults were put on show. We learned not to judge each other and found new ways of living honestly.

I spent nights on the edge of fear of what was to happen to us. The valuation report had come back and the property which we had been advised could be worth as much as 1.2 Million pounds was now valued at £900,000. A market slump had occurred since we had purchased it as Tannery House and had devalued it significantly. The Good Doctor and his partner were no longer interested in The Lighthouse, and the relationship which was already strained now became even worse.

I was starting to feel very alone in my mind. How were we to survive let alone to purchase this property and follow the guidance!

Leave everything and follow me!

Not this again! What else is there to leave now?

The Car!

Living with God

I had left my wife with two cars and taken my joy with me which was an old Jaguar sports car, not worth much, but I loved it. She had been sitting in the drive for many weeks and I was unable to afford to run her. We had been using a small Renault that belonged to the Angel, and the car payments were well behind.

By now all thought of holding on to the Jaguar was of little interest, food was more important and the bills were growing without means of paying them. I advertised the Jaguar on e-bay and quickly sold her for £3000.00 a lot less than I had paid in recent months for her repairs. Right now though, this money was like a king's ransom. We settled some of the urgent debts and the three of us ate well for a short time.

We all thanked God for this prosperous financial intervention at a very difficult time.

The spiritual education continued relentlessly. We were being prepared to become of use to others as we faced all of our own demons and defects. Christmas was approaching, and now everyone who had once supported us no longer kept contact. Our American friend and the community we had come to know there no longer communicated with us.

The knives were out as discussions were being held by others about our staying in the property instead of selling it. People who had called themselves friends disappeared without trace. We were alone without friends or family. The Good Doctor approached me once more asking if I would leave the property as and when a sale was completed. I advised him that as an officer of what was Tannery House Ltd it was my fiduciary duty not to get in the way of the proper procedure of sale. I would of course vacate. Throughout all this my guidance was still the same, I was to purchase the property, and I accepted that only God knew how.

The Angel, Patrick and I became closer and closer as others closed ranks against us.

Stay in the love. Just be, and all will be well!

The word be and being had taken on new meaning for us staying honest in all our affairs, judging no one, accepting that our lives were in God's hands whatever God's will was for us. It did not stop the tiger that whispered in my ear, the tiger of doubt that was waiting to pounce on any thought that entered my mind of disbelief or doubt and tear my process to pieces, that demon "fear" wishing only to return me to the inner solitude of my previous self. I have and still do see that tiger sitting waiting, forever watchful, for any weakness.

This message came to us daily. Our one remaining supporter who was living in The Lighthouse was starting to loose faith. Some of the lessons we were getting were becoming ones that he did not wish to learn at that time. One afternoon while I was sitting in meditation, Sananda came to me and said.

You are to put on a course. It will be for ten people. It will be called The Awakening. It will be a journey into self, and it will be for three weeks commencing on the 16th of January 2005.

Living with God

Panic!

My mind immediately clogged up with the logistics of such a course. How? What are we to teach? Where will they all sleep? What will they sleep on? No beds... How will we provide food for them? How will we cook it? There was not even a cooker or a chair to sit on in The Lighthouse. Where will these people come from? Everyone we knew had deserted The Lighthouse and vacated any friendship they had with us.

Have faith and all you need will be provided!

I told the Angel and Patrick of the guidance. Like me they both jumped to the same conclusions. I told them that I was to speak with Sananda again soon for further details. All three of us spent the night fighting the disbelief. We could not even feed ourselves, and we were being told to put on a three week residential course about a journey into self UGH! We had been told that we would purchase The Lighthouse, and that all we needed would be provided. Nothing seemed further from what was our reality.

Several things we were told were not happening. We were now stretched beyond our known levels of faith. It would have been so easy for all of us to pack up and run. To everyone outside we were crazy, totally lost in some fantasy world. Some were saying that I was channelling darkness, evil spirits that just wanted to hurt people.

Those who were in the council had chosen a route of the destruction of us rather than facing themselves.

Christmas came and went and nothing! No news of the course. The three of us celebrated Christmas together simply, forgetting the pressures of the bills and the material lack that we were in. All of the problems fizzled out of our minds as we were joined by a new arrival, **Finnegan.** My Angel and I had talked on many occasions of one day getting ourselves a dog. We had even discussed the issue with Sananda, who had confirmed the future arrival of a dog that would be named Finnegan. We were bowled over when days before Christmas we were gifted a ten week old, long legged floppy ball of love in the form of a boxer puppy. His skin sagged from his body like he was wearing an overcoat that belonged to his father, wrinkles of skin hanging round his feet waiting for him to grow into it, big brown eyes that looked right into your heart and melted it. God had given us a warm loving creature that would become a great teacher to all of us, especially in the art of unconditional love.

The love that had grown between the three of us, now four, made sure that even in our isolation we had each other. We all knew that God would, if sought, help us.

Bailiffs were knocking at the door now with increasing regularity, each trying to seize assets to settle the debts and each walking away empty handed. There was nothing to take, no stick of furniture or item worth selling.

The Inland Revenue joined the queue visiting me to collect £1800 in unpaid taxes. The inspector and I sat together to discus the matter. All I had were the clothes I was standing in. Reluctantly she left empty handed.

Living with God

New Year was celebrated together looking forward to what was to come. For the first time in my life I remember wishing for nothing more than what I was now deeply immersed in.

Love in a greater abundance than my body and mind could take in.

I spent many hours watching the Angel sleep peacefully next to me; I admired her courage and unbending faith. Her life had been difficult, and she had triumphed over the events that would turn the strongest of people into socially corrupt beings.

She was showing me how to live my life. I loved her so much in that silence of each night when I looked at her.

In previous years, especially at this time of year, I had many of my character defects hitting me. Jealousy of what others had and what I had not, the love that was openly displayed, and that seemed more prevalent at this time of year than others, money, materialism and selfish wants, but these things no longer seemed to be a necessary part of my life.

For once I had nothing material, and yet I was the richest man in the kingdom.

Chapter 11

Trust

I was feeling comfortable in my own skin for the first time feeling the pleasure of letting go and trusting this new found friend and teacher, Sananda. My love for this energy was growing beyond my ability to understand the non physical. It was now Sunday the 9th of January 2005. I had until now no further guidance on the course at all.

As I sat in meditation alone, Sananda came to me again.

Blessings my beloved. You are to contact the following and invite them here for the course!

I was given a list of names in Denmark and England to contact.

You will fly to Denmark and tell these people of The Awakening. You will charge them the figure that I give you to attend. You will return with the money to provide the needs for this course. One person from England will come on this course free of charge; it is our gift to her!

Surprised I noted the list given. The people from Denmark listed by Sananda were people I hardly knew, and I had worked with them very tenuously before, and now I was to ask them to come to England for three weeks and to leave everything that their lives were in less than 5 days. On top of this they were to pay not an insignificant amount of money.

Make haste on this journey. You have much to do!

What? All of this seems impossible! What about everything else that is needed here to facilitate this course, beds and...............

Be!!!!!!!!!!!!! Everything you need will be provided! Accept our commission. Have faith. We will not forsake you. We will send you an angel to help.

My mind was reeling. How the hell was this course going to happen? Even if these people that I was guided to invite wanted to come, the cost, the logistics, my mind couldn't cope. All I could do was follow.

I left the meditation room in a state of shock; I was unable to consider that all of this was possible. After telling the Angel and Patrick of the guidance, they both stared at me bemused. Well, what have we got to lose? They both chimed. I accepted that it would all turn out as it was meant to be and started the process by telephoning one of the people on the list that Sananda had given me, a lady who lived in Denmark. She was a kind lady full of the best intent. She was in her early sixties and had become a good friend on my frequent journeys to her country in the past. She had been involved in helping to make arrangements for the lectures I often gave.

I had never had a mother in the true sense of the word. This lady was a warm comforting person who had shown a motherly care that I had never felt in many years. She had taken on a role as my surrogate parent and often acted like my mother on many occasions. When I spoke to her, I told her of my guidance from Sananda, and she agreed to get everyone together in her apartment in Copenhagen ready for my flying visit.

The three of us had difficulty believing what was happening. Within the hour I was booked on a flight for the following morning to Copenhagen without the money to get back.

We had spent every last penny we had to do this. It was the last of everything that had kept us from complete poverty. We were in God's hands as to what the outcome of this journey would be.

The next morning I packed a few small items, toothbrush, (no toothpaste, to take what was there would leave the

Angel with none, and I had to rely on using someone else's property), a clean shirt, razor and little else. Feeling very nervous and at the mercy of God I said goodbye to my Angel and Patrick.

Totally trusting, my head full of the image of my Angel and Patrick as I left. Their eyes were full of love and respect as I drove out of the gates to the airport.

I had travelled the world in my previous life experience, but never without even the means for a cup of tea. Life had been lived high on the hog, eating in fancy restaurants, sitting in private lounges in the airports awaiting my flights. I felt very different now as I looked at the people in the airport doing what people do; eating, chatting, reading, browsing in shops, I was aware of how different my life had become. The flight was short, but it seemed to take forever. My mind was racing. The tiger in my mind had me. All of my fears were running riot. These people would think me completely mad.

My sleeping ego had surfaced. Me who was once a professional businessman was now reduced to hare-brained schemes that at best were from a mind completely lost in fantasy or at worst a mind that was lost to all reality, insane. My future was definitely in God's hands. Whatever happened from here on in was not under my control. I fought with myself for the rest of the journey; God did this, not me. He was the one who sent me. I wasn't mad. My nerves were in tatters; fear rose and fell within me time and again like a roller coaster throughout the flight. I was a shivering wreck as we approached Copenhagen airport. Was this all going to turn out to be a bad dream?

Raven

I was met at the airport by my surrogate parent this kind lady. It was good to feel the warmth of her smile. Outside of the company of the angel and Patrick it felt like everyone else in the world was full of hostility towards me. We sat and chatted for a while in the airport café, talking of the reason for my journey. As I told her the whole story, I saw the look on her face change as she started to understand exactly what I was suggesting. A deep frown furrowed her brow as she tried to break it gently to me, it would be impossible for these people I had asked to see to drop everything and come to England for three weeks at short notice, even if they had wanted to, She said all is not lost. At least we can have a pleasant evening together. My confidence was knocked a little more as we walked out of the airport together and drove to her apartment in central Copenhagen.

That night I didn't rest. I was on the edge all night. My mind created all sorts of different outcomes to my visit from how idiotic this was to flights of fancy that took me into wild dreams of impossible futures.

The morning finally came. I lay watching the darkness of the night disappearing as the first hint of sunrise came up behind the cloudy sky creating a half light that seemed as though it really did not want to be there that day, just like me.

I wanted to be somewhere else, not to have to face the events of today. Why could my life not be simpler than this? Other people had planned lives that seemed so easy. How much I wanted to be in a factory job right then, "to be normal" with my life completely planned out for me, to live to three score and ten, (if lucky) and die without the world

Living with God

ever knowing I had existed. I was living what I had asked for right now, free of the restrictions of the past. But in that moment I was just like a child that wants one thing and complains heavily till it gets it, and when it does, it is still not satisfied and continues harping on wanting to change yet again. God was teaching me invaluable lessons every step of the way through this trip, I smiled at myself as I caught these negative childish thoughts creeping through my mind. I was here to do a job, and I would get on with it with a smile on my face, whatever the results were.

After a typical Danish breakfast with my friend of cheese, jam and bread I told her that I needed to take a walk around the lakes in front of her apartment to prepare myself for our visitors. She still had the look of deep concern on her face. As she hugged me, she had indicated to me how deluded I had become with the machinations of my mind that were taking me down a path of personal disaster. In her mind the world just did not share the fantasy that she considered I was living in.

I left her clearing up the breakfast table and took myself out into the cold Scandinavian air; the lakes were frozen, with swans sitting on the ice staring at me as I slowly walked past them trying to clear my mind. I had no idea what I was going to say or do, or what type of reception I would be greeted with by these people. I gave up again and said out loud, "God, I am at your mercy". I was powerless. Accepting this I walked back, pleased to feel the warmth as I entered the apartment block. Copenhagen in winter was unforgiving to those who were not prepared for it, and I didn't own a coat at that time.

Raven

As I entered the apartment, I felt a shiver run up my spine. Everyone that I had asked to come was already there. They were early, sitting on settees in the lounge, lined up like naughty schoolchildren waiting for the headmaster, all very quiet and eager to hear why they had been asked to attend at such short notice. My mouth was dry, and after a warm greeting from them I sat down on the floor in front of them and waited, I didn't know how to handle this, so I waited for Sananda.

Each face in front of me was full of looks of apprehension. They were searching my eyes for signs or clues to understand the moment, but my eyes, face and body were vacant and gave them nothing. I had let go of control, and they could not fathom what was going on. I felt the energy of Sananda rise within me as I faded more and more from the scene. Abruptly a voice that was not mine came from my body and a startled look came over the faces of all present as the voice of Sananda went on to say.

All of you are here because you have asked for freedom, freedom from the way that your life has developed. We have come because you asked us for help. We have heard your prayers. Over the next three weeks you will have the opportunity to end your suffering. Are you prepared to journey into yourself, to look at yourself completely, to see the darkness within, remove it, and allow the light of God to enter you fully, bringing peace, freedom and love into your hearts?

This was the first time Sananda had ever spoken to some of them and for others it was the first time they had ever heard spirit at all. A stunned silence hung in the room. No one spoke for what seemed an eternity. This small group of Danes were being offered God's grace, and they wanted and needed it. Tears appeared in some of their eyes, looks of bewilderment came over others. One of them said
"I have been praying for so long and now here is the answer". She broke down in tears as Sananda spoke again.

The weight of your soul lies heavy in your hearts, burdened with the disease that all humanity carries. Take courage. Open your hearts to God and you will be free.

Sananda left my body, and the whole group sat in silence including me. I was left to explain what had been said to them, what God wanted for them all, and I proceeded to tell them of the course that was starting in England the following Monday, This was now only 5 days away. I was faced with a barrage of questions, none of which I could answer questions like what was going to happen. I didn't know!
All I knew was that God was in charge and everything that was going to happen was in God's hands, they would have to put their trust in God.

Raven

The group sat talking to each other. Questions were being thrown around the room rapidly building the excitement to a fever pitch. Between them they were solving each others problems that would stop them from coming like who will take care of my dog? "My sister", another answered. I don't have any holiday entitlement left said another. What was more important was the cry from several others. I decided to leave them to their own deliberations and left the room to join my friend in the kitchen. I had done all that was necessary. I had turned up and delivered the message. My job was over.

My friend looked at me as I entered the kitchen. Her face still carried the deep frowns of concern. She knew what had been said, but like a mother who did not wish to see the disappointment in her child as its plans were dashed on the rocks of failure, she filled the kettle and tried to offer me comfort in her kind words. I was totally relieved; my burden had been lifted like a heavy cloud that had engulfed my whole body all through the previous sleepless night. We sat chatting together in her kitchen over a cup of Earl grey tea, (sadly PG Tips has still not made it into Denmark), our conversation was idly wending its way through a forest of insignificant recollections of times from the past, times that we had shared together on this lecture tour or that visit to Odense. We were interrupted by the woman who had her prayers answered when she heard the message from Sananda, "We have all decided to come", she said. Her words shot out into the air like unguided missiles full of excitement. I saw the look on my friend's face change. Her chin hit the floor in disbelief.

Living with God

All of them decided to come. It did not matter what the obstacles were They would face their immediate demons like fears of flying, lack of money, leaving the dog, getting unscheduled time off work, all manner of other things, but they were coming. None of them wanted to miss the chance of receiving this grace and freedom that Sananda had promised them.

I was astounded at this response. Never in a million years would I have considered that this could happen. I went back into the room where the excited group was still gathered and gave them all instructions on the next steps to be taken by them. As I finished they flew into action, detailing tasks to each other like flight bookings, transport to the airport, meeting places etc. The chatter continued as they all filed out of the apartment, one of them telling me they would return with the money for the course later that day and that they all were looking forward to seeing me in England.

I left for England the next day. I was grateful to my friend who had helped me to get this organised so quickly. She left me at the check in desk in Copenhagen Airport, happy that things had worked out so well, telling me that she was also looking forward to being with us in our centre the following week. My pockets were full of money, deposits that people had paid me for the course. Some of it paid for my ticket home.

I felt more fear in me now, than I had before I came. God had told me what to do, and I had followed. The most incredible thing that my mind was struggling with was that it had all happened as God had said it would. My fear was growing, because now all of these people had accepted God's invitation and paid the money and I did not have a clue what was going on. I just felt a huge burden being placed on my shoulders. Little did I know I was putting it there myself.

The burden is not yours to carry. Get your ego out of the way. This is our course, not yours. We will be the guides and teachers that deliver this grace.

I was letting myself get in the way. This was God's course and all I had to do was trust and turn up as always, but what about all the other things that were needed at The Lighthouse to facilitate this course? You said you would send us an angel to help. Well?

Have faith. Believe in us. All that we have said will come to pass.

I still had difficulty accepting that this ethereal voice in my head was real. What I did know was that it seemed to be right, so I comforted myself with the thought that all was as it should be.

My Angel and Patrick were waiting eagerly for me when I returned. I excitedly told them everything that had happened and showed them the pockets full of money. It felt as if our world was starting to change, we could eat and pay some long overdue bills. We laughed with each other. It was the type of laughing that is uncontrollable, a very nervous laughter which often happens when tears may fit the bill better.

That afternoon all three of us sat in the small cottage in the grounds of The Lighthouse and talked about what had to be done in the next three days. There was so much to be done. More fear arose in us. Could it be possible to achieve it all in so little time?

As we sat talking I noticed a small Indian looking woman entering the gates of the centre. I walked out of the cottage to greet her. We often had people coming in for all types of reasons, some just because they heard the building was for sale and wanted a snoop. What this lady wanted I didn't know. She introduced herself speaking with a very pleasant upper class English accent. She was asking for somewhere to store furniture and had heard we might be able to help.

I sat and talked with her as she described to me in detail what had befallen her husband and herself. They had been forced to downsize from a large manor house to a small cottage and had a large excess of furniture they were unable to use. Bad times had hit her and her husband. They had lost their business, home, income and were in trouble. They hadn't the money to live.

Invite her and her work colleagues here for the first week of the course. They will be needed to facilitate the first part of The Awakening.

Sananda was talking to me as though he was present at all my conversations and gave me instant guidance without me having to sit and wait for answers to the questions I asked. I was starting to learn not to question but to follow. I asked her what she did, and she told me that she was a Reflexologist and masseuse.

I was not surprised., This was God at work, and I told her of what was happening from Monday of the following week, and that there would be 10 course members who would need to receive both of her skills each day; ten full body massages and ten foot massages per day for five days. She smiled saying that she could not possibly fulfil that herself but she could and would organise a team of women to help her. In an instant two of the problems we were facing were solved. We quickly agreed a price for the furniture she needed to be rid of and the massages that she and her team would supply on the course. It was amazing to look at the list of items this couple needed to sell. Everything fitted our needs perfectly. It was as if we had written the list of furniture requirements ourselves, and they had been delivered from a furniture warehouse everything from chairs to beds, tables and carpets, and their was even a set of African drums. I felt great pleasure in being able to help this woman from the good fortune that God had brought to us. I saw a look of relief cover her face as this changed her situation, even if only momentarily, and she hurried away very pleased with her day's achievements. Now she too had a pocket full of money.

The Angel, Patrick and I were reeling at the speed with which God brought things into manifestation so quickly. The first week of the course was forming in our minds and The Lighthouse had just been furnished with everything we needed to facilitate the course, as if someone had waved a magic wand. Over the next three days we worked like dogs.

Many things had to be done, purchasing bedding, food, hiring a minibus to collect our guests and transport us all around for the next three weeks. By late on the Saturday night we had finished. Everything was in place.

A bloody Miracle!!!

We had all been part of a miracle, watching it actually evolve in front of us. We sat together laughing and talking late into the night, all three of us feeling happier than we had done for a long time. We had a course, and some of our hard work was being rewarded. We had settled nearly all our bills and could breathe again for a short time.

Sunday morning came all too quickly. With a slight feeling of apprehension, Patrick and I drove to Stansted Airport to collect our guests. Were they going to appear? This had all happened so fast. We wondered whether they had been able to do all the things they needed to, to be able to come. It would have been totally reasonable for them not to. No need for excuses; it was a near impossible task. I was expecting at least some of them to have cancelled. I was wrong. On arriving I found them all standing waiting with baggage and all. The small group huddled closely together, aliens in England looking very sheepish.

I felt a real surge of admiration for them. They had come to face their personal demons and change their lives at the drop of a hat. It took courage. I have often asked myself since. Would I have had the courage to do what they were committing themselves to? They taught me another step in the valuable lesson of trust. All of them were displaying trust beyond normal to have come, and I felt humbled by them.

As Patrick and I approached the group, we saw the relief come on their faces. Frowns were replaced with smiles as they saw someone they knew walking toward them. They had come from Copenhagen main international airport, which even on its busiest days was like taking a walk in an empty park compared to the level of human movement they were seeing here. The airport arrivals hall was heaving with people, all struggling and pushing against each other to find a better place close to the exit point of the immigration control where their loved ones would emerge, struggling with baggage carts that seemed to want to go in the opposite direction to the way that the weary passenger wished to go, their faces showing the level of distress. Our group had made it through this melee safely and we could rescue them from this Sunday afternoon madness.

We packed our small group into the minibus and left the bedlam of the airport well behind us. The peace was short lived, as we took the exit from the relatively quiet M11 on to the tortuous journey around the M25 towards the M3. These people were used to quiet motorways; five million people inhabited the whole of their country compared with the sixty five million plus people squashed into this tiny space called Britain. I watched the faces of my passengers in the rear view mirror as I drove, wincing and whooping as another driver in a car that was going far too fast screamed past us dodging in and out of the overcrowded lanes of traffic late for work or his next appointment, and demonstrating the overall reality of the stress levels of most people that lived in this country.

Our guests had never seen anything like this. It was busier than the famous Tivoli Gardens on New Years Eve and a lot more dangerous than any rollercoaster ride they had ever been on.

Chapter 12

The Awakening

We managed to negotiate our way safely back to the rural peace of our village after a gentle meander through the New Forest. It was a pleasant change driving through the miles of unspoilt countryside filled with deer and wild horses, a complete contrast to seeing the craziness of a country at work with people racing madly in every direction. What they had witnessed on the drive was now forgotten and replaced with the calming effects of Britain's countryside at its best. We pulled into the sanctuary of The Lighthouse, taking in a deep breath and feeling like a major triumph had been achieved. My Angel was standing at the cottage door waiting to greet us. I felt my heart melt as I looked at her standing tall and beautiful. The rest of that day was spent settling into the new surroundings that were to be home for the next three weeks. Rooms were allocated and the general details of safety and certain rules that needed to be adhered to,

Living with God

were explained to the group, now complete with the Danish and English course members all together.

That first afternoon we sat together in the main meditation room, the room that was once the main treatment room of our old clinic. The only items of furniture or comfort in the room were a collection of different coloured and sized cushions that we had collected for the group to sit on. This was where we would spend many hours together in the coming weeks.

We handed out gifts to all our guests at this meeting, a recital of the Desiderata framed for them to have in their rooms while with us, and to take home after the course, and a silver chain with the Indian sign of the Ohm (The Universal Sound) hanging from it. I had been guided to give each course member a copy of a document that had been published on the internet called "The Awakening" and to my knowledge is not attributed to any named author. When I first read this paper, I was astounded, as it carried the same name as the course we were running, and it seemed to say everything about the issues that we were addressing within us. Certainly no coincidence. (A message from God).

The Awakening
Author unknown

A time comes in your life when you finally get it...When in the midst of all your fears and insanity, you stop dead in your tracks and somewhere the voice inside your head cries out ENOUGH! Enough fighting and crying or struggling to hold on. And, like a child quieting down after a blind tantrum, your sobs begin to subside, you shudder once or twice, you blink back your tears and through a mantle of wet lashes, you begin to look at the world through new eyes.

This is your awakening. You realize that it's time to stop hoping and waiting for something to change or for happiness, safety and security to come galloping over the next horizon. You come to terms with the fact that I am not Prince Charming and you are not Cinderella and that in the real world there aren't always fairy tale endings (or beginnings for that matter) and that any guarantee of "happily ever after" must begin with you.

You awaken to the fact that you are not perfect and that not everyone will always love, appreciate or approve of who

Living with God

or what you are... and that's OK. (They are entitled to their own views and opinions.) And you learn the importance of loving and championing yourself and in the process, a sense of new found confidence is born of self-approval.

You stop blaming other people for the things they did to you (or didn't do for you), and you learn that the only thing you can really count on is the unexpected. You learn that people don't always say what they mean or mean what they say and that not everyone will always be there for you, and that it's not always about you. So you learn to stand on your own and to take care of yourself and in the process a sense of safety and security is born of self-reliance.

You stop judging and pointing fingers and you begin to accept people as they are and to overlook their shortcomings and human frailties and in the process, a sense of peace and contentment is born of forgiveness.

You realise that much of the way you view yourself and the world around you, is as a result of all the messages and opinions that have been ingrained into your thick head. And you begin to sift through all the crap you've been fed about how you should behave, how you should look and how much you should weigh, what you should wear and where you should shop and what you should drive, how and where you should live and what you should do for a living, who you should marry and what you should expect of a marriage, the importance of having and raising children or what you owe your parents.

You learn to open up to new worlds and different points of view. And you begin reassessing and redefining who you are and what you really stand for. You learn the difference between wanting and needing and you begin to discard the doctrines and values you've outgrown, or should never have bought in to to begin with, and in the process you learn to go with your instincts.

You learn that it is truly in giving that we receive. And that there is power and glory in creating and contributing, and you stop manoeuvring through life merely as a "consumer" looking for your next fix. You learn that principles such as honesty and integrity are not the outdated ideals of a bygone era but the mortar that holds together the foundation upon which you must build a life.

You learn that you don't know everything, it's not your job to save the world and that you can't teach a pig to sing. You learn to distinguish between guilt and responsibility and the importance of setting boundaries and learning to say no. You learn that the only cross to bear is the one you choose to carry and that martyrs get burned at the stake.

Then you learn about love. Romantic love and familial love. How to love, how much to give in love, when to stop giving and when to walk away. You learn not to project you needs or your feelings onto a relationship. You learn that you will not be more beautiful, more intelligent, more loveable or important because of the man on your arm or the child that bears your name. You learn to look at relationships as they really are and not as you would have them be.

You stop trying to control people, situations and outcomes. You learn that just as people grow and change so it is with love...And you learn that you don't have the right to demand love on your terms...Just to make you happy. And, you learn that alone does not mean lonely... And you look in the mirror

Living with God

and come to terms with the fact that you will never be a size 5 or a perfect 10 and you stop trying to compete with the image inside your head and agonizing over how you "stack up".

You also stop working so hard at putting your feelings aside, smoothing things over and ignoring your needs. You learn that feelings of entitlement are perfectly OK...And that it is your right to want things and to ask for the things that you want. And that sometimes it is necessary to make demands. You come to the realization that you deserve to be treated with love, kindness, sensitivity and respect and you won't settle for less. And, you allow only the hands of a lover who cherishes you to glorify you with his touch... and in the process you internalize the meaning of self-respect.

And you learn that your body really is your temple. And you begin to care for it and treat it with respect. You begin eating a balanced diet, drinking more water and taking more time to exercise. You learn that fatigue diminishes the spirit and can create doubt and fear. So you take more time to rest. And, just as food fuels the body, laughter fuels our soul. So, you take more time to laugh and to play. You learn that for the most part in life, you get what you believe you deserve... and that much of life is truly a self-fulfilling prophecy.

You learn that anything worth achieving is worth working for, and that wishing for something to happen is different from working towards making it happen. More importantly, you learn that in order to achieve success you need direction, discipline and perseverance. You also learn that no one can do it all alone, and that it's OK to risk asking for help. You learn that the only thing you must truly fear is the great robber baron of all time, FEAR itself. You learn to step right into and through your fears because you know that whatever happens you can handle it and to give in to fear is to give away the right to live life on your terms. And you learn to fight for your life and not to squander it living under a cloud of impending doom.

You learn that life isn't always fair, you don't always get what you think you deserve, and that sometimes bad things happen to unsuspecting, good people. On these occasions you learn not to personalize things. You learn that God isn't punishing you or failing to answer you prayers. It's just life happening. And you learn to deal with evil in its most primal state. The ego. You learn that negative feelings such as anger, envy and resentment must be understood and redirected or they will suffocate the life out of you and poison the universe that surrounds you. You learn to admit when you are wrong and to build bridges instead of walls.

You learn to be thankful and to take comfort in many of the simple things we take for granted, things that millions of people upon the earth can only dream about; a full refrigerator, clean running water, a soft warm bed, a long hot shower. Slowly, you begin to take responsibility for yourself by yourself and you make yourself a promise to never betray yourself and to never settle for less than your heart's desire. And you hang a wind chime outside you window so you can listen to the wind. And you make it a point to keep smiling, to keep trusting and to stay open to every wonderful possibility. Finally, with courage in your heart and with God by your side, you take a stand, you take a deep breath and you begin to design the life you want to live as best you can.

Living with God

Everyone present read this and without exception had a real feeling that they were in the right place, because what was written certainly applied to all of us.

We finished our brief meeting with an evening meal taken together in the dining room, as all meals would be from now on. We would cook, clean, eat and sleep together from now on. The day finally ended with advice that yoga practice would be taken by all of us together each morning at 7.00 am. This announcement was met with a slight groan by certain members who had not anticipated any physical challenges. The Angel and I left for the peace of our one roomed cottage with relief pouring from us. Happily tired, we slept in each others arms all night.

The first day of the course started as promised with the 7.00 am yoga practice taken by my Angel. Groaning, creaking bodies were given a chance to breathe again as parts of our unused systems were gently awoken after many years slumbering. This practice was the prelude to the whole week which was all about physical detoxification and relaxation. Our bodies needed to be ready to support the mental and emotional work that was to come later.

Throughout that first day, following a healthy stretching start and a hearty breakfast, the group was to go through a regime of foot massage, full body massage and meditation. We were introduced to drinking several freshly squeezed fruit and vegetable juices, two coffee enemas (that is introducing a coffee solution through the rectum to cleanse the liver and colon. Highly recommended), one-to- one channelling with Sananda, two hearty vegetarian meals with the ingredients coming from good organic sources, home cooked and much more. The process was very hard for most people who had just not been used to looking after themselves and were used to the poor food they ate every day, the lack of exercise, lack of relaxation and so on.

Bodies started to let go of more than they were expecting. This process continued for the whole of the first week.

That first week of the course was a great success. Everyone settled into a new healthy way of living, new relationships were being formed amongst the group and an easy atmosphere had developed.

The group knitted together like a new family each showing positive different sides of themselves, but as the end of the week approached, I was becoming nervous again. What was to happen next week? I had no idea. Fear was building within me. My ego was starting to get in the way again. This was my responsibility, and my trust in God was fading fast the closer the end came.

It was the Friday night of the first week, and the massages were over. Everyone was feeling slightly nervous. This was the first time they had ever allowed themselves to relax to such an extent.

The week had been a challenge for all of us, but enjoyable.

As the week came to its close, things started to change. Raw emotions began to be released by many of the group members as their bodies eased from the stressful busy lives accepted by all of us as normal.

Tears, anger, jealousy, opinions, gossip, judgements, control, fear, the whole myriad of human emotions were starting to show amongst the group. It was as though a tap

Living with God

had been turned on within each and every person, allowing their true nature to emerge. Sparks were starting to fly as the masks that we all wore in our day-to-day lives were being slowly removed, and we were starting to awaken to our true selves.

The Awakening had really started, I realised as did everyone else that what we had all committed ourselves to was not for the faint hearted. For some feelings of fear had started to become so great that the desire to run was becoming a real consideration. We had all been hiding from ourselves for so long. Just being massaged, relaxing and living together had sparked so much. A real fear of the unknown was growing. Some of us did not want to see anymore of ourselves. We certainly did not want any more of our soft underbellies to be seen by others.

Over that first weekend we continued with work that was all guided by spirit, shamanic energy clearing, venturing into nature, doing things that these people had never thought they would.

The crutches of life had been removed, and it was showing. Over our lives some of us had used alcohol, drugs of all kinds and other emotional crutches to support us through the day. All of these had been removed for this course, and as the time went by, cracks were appearing within the members of the group and within the group as a whole. A division had appeared that was starting to become nasty.

Everything is perfect!

Raven

In a quiet moment I had sought council with Sananda. Everything felt like it was falling apart, and I was going to have a war on my hands. Everything looked like a complete mess to me. This was not what we expected. What am I to do? I was afraid that something or someone was going to explode.

What did you expect?

This is the awakening we promised. All that is happening is perfect! You are all being awoken to yourselves. Seeing the true self is painful and yet glorious, for in seeing yourself, you can start to make choices as to whether you change it or not. The greatest gift from God is the freedom of choice. The reason for all dysfunction in your lives, all disharmonies is now being displayed within the group. All of you are suffering from diseases that man's medicine cannot remedy. Every disease that man suffers; mental, emotional and physical, is heavily impacted by spiritual disease, which is a spiritual void within. That void is increasing daily. You and many others have asked why such things as cancer, heart disease, mental disorders, drug abuse, and all manner of other diseases are increasing within God's world. Man is destroying himself, as always by seeking only chemical answers, to issues that are only too often spiritual problems. The principal of wishing to help others by such discoveries of new drugs is admirable, but helping others is no longer the primary driving force behind the use of drugs for disease. Greed, financial gain, controls, these are the forces behind the drugs that are being peddled, skulking behind the well meaning people, like your doctors and nurses who use them as the cover that hides the dark forces that drive the medical system within your world. These are the forces that are destroying man. It is only when man accepts the spiritual void within himself and looks to heal that, that healing from a great many of these physical, mental, and emotional diseases can be helped. It is only then that man's creativity, his knowledge and learning, can start to have a greater impact on his fellows. Many disease states will never change dramatically until the sufferer accepts himself fully; all of his character defects are increasing the spiritual void within him. It is all these defects that draw man away from God and into disease. Heal the spirit as well as the body and mind.

So you see everything is perfect! All of you are seeing yourselves, your character defects, the defects that create your spiritual void and increase your physical maladies. As always you now have the answers to help cure them. Follow me and all will be well. Have faith and trust in God and we will not forsake you! Change these character defects for positive loving actions, thoughts, words and deeds. Give of yourself to others without looking for personal gain and God will heal you. The almighty created you and the almighty can heal you! It is you that have to take the steps towards healing. Is your life bad enough that you are now completely ready for God to remove these defects? Are you ready to take the action needed to become free?

Am I hearing you right? Many of the diseases that man suffers are exacerbated by a spiritual disease, a spiritual void within?

Emphatically Yes! Man is living in disease, Dis-ease, not at ease with himself spiritually because of all the character defects he suffers, he is living in "Attention", at-tension unable to free himself from pain through his inability to look inwards at himself for some of the missing answers to his ailments. Living at-tension locks the body mind and spirit. When these parts of self are locked, nothing can flow When you are not flowing, you stagnate and become dis-eased.

What about the other factors like poor diet, hereditary disease, exposure to dangerous chemicals and so many other things? What a field day the medical profession will have with your question. They will say what rubbish! They say they have scientific evidence to prove what causes disease.

Let Them! Arrogance has never served a positive purpose. Who are we to change what God has given man, the freedom of choice, to decide what to believe or disbelieve? Those who choose to look into themselves, to see the true nature of what and who they have become, accept it, change it and seek God's help. They will know the truth. When man stops creating his own spiritual void then he will start the real road to healing. It is after this action that man's drugs may be of better use to the needy. Disease will only increase without taking this action, and it is an action that each individual must take, not something he can be given or purchase. It is the inner work for which we are all personally responsible. It is the hardest thing we will ever do and only we can do it. Once accepted, it is the easiest fastest cure. Once man accepts this fact, then he has his own ability to change his future!

So if I understand what you are saying, it is the spiritual void that is created within us, which is what I am witnessing in the group right now, control, jealousy, opinions, gossip, condemnation, deceit, lying, manipulation, resentment and that it is these things that create the void and are drawing us away from the sunlight of the spirit, blocking us from God and helping to increase the level of disease?

In simple terms, yes!

This is going to create a stir!

These are the crosses that man bears, the crosses that are your own responsibility. no one else can carry them for you. Man will never be rid of these defects entirely. Your journey is to learn mastery of them, to keep them under control so that they no longer eat away at you, so that they no longer rule your experience, creating pain. As soon as they are not safely mastered then dis-ease comes back, disease of all kinds. Once mastered, freedom from nearly all of man's pains can be achieved.

Living with God

Thank you for this opportunity, but it is bloody hard to do this. What are we to do next in this coming week of The Awakening? How can I stop this from getting out of hand with those explosions occurring in the group?

Let it explode! When an explosion occurs, all that was is now fragmented. A new beginning can take place for those who choose to take courage and journey into themselves to see all that they are. Follow the guidance. Let the explosions happen. To stop them or try to pacify yourselves will deny you the opportunity of growth. In the coming week all will find a new path to walk which will deliver all the abundance that you have been promised.

This was fantastic, but I was feeling very scared. During the following two weeks we were all engaged looking deeply into ourselves. We fought and fought with what we saw, not wanting to accept what we encountered within.

Some of the group started to run to old crutches like alcohol, some started to create and look for excuses as to why this course could not possibly work for them, what horseshit was this anyway I heard them say, our lives, our diseases, our problems, were all someone else's fault!

It was truly amazing to witness and to see the lengths that we will all go to in order to avoid accepting responsibility for our ills, indeed for ourselves.

Even the bravest struggled, but for those who persevered, the rewards came fast and furious.

Dependency on people, places and things (outside of God and ourselves) started to disappear. The need for materialism and other crutches were gradually forgotten. We learned that we were full of fear and that fear was the catalyst to our problems.

The diseases that we were suffering stopped in an instant. For some of these people where every type of medical intervention had failed, and for some this had been over very long periods, perhaps, ten to twenty years. God was now showing us the miracles of working with ourselves and showing us the power of living with God. When we started to learn mastery of these inner issues, we started to experience what life could be like 'living with God'.

God is within all man. You have to look no further than yourself in order to see. Man is made in the image of God, and the kingdom of heaven is available for all to experience here on earth. It is within you. Not in your churches, mosques or other places of worship. Learn to love yourself, and by doing so, you will learn to master fear, to live with God, and as you do so, so shall you learn to live with each other, loving each other free of all that has pained you, in peace freedom and harmony.

Miraculously everyone stayed the course. As the end loomed we saw that everything had worked out better than any of us could ever had imagined. For most of us we had received the gift of peace, freedom and love that we had been promised; free from ills that had been with us for so many years.

A couple of the members of the group had not allowed themselves the freedom of seeing themselves properly, and by their own admissions were quite happy to stay as they were. God will give them another opportunity. I have learned that life is one constant opportunity. I have not liked the way it has been presented sometimes. In fact, I have hated it! However, since changing my perspective on my life's events, changing my view of them from tragedies to opportunities, everything seems to be far more acceptable.

Life just seems to flow more easily. Blocks have stopped within me by accepting whatever happens as God's will for me, and that it is perfect. I feel as if I have become like a reed on a river bank bending with the wind and the flow of the river, letting it all pass through and around me, not letting emotions and events clog up my system, causing me pain and dis-ease.

Our small group had been on an amazing journey. Without exception we had all had life changing experiences. We felt sad to see them all go, but happy and excited at the prospect of the new lives we were all heading towards.

I took time alone again and thanked Sananda for the lessons I had learned, for the opportunities God had given us all. What had taken place was a miracle. It had all flowed like a well oiled slick operation that had been worked out by a real professional training team, no gaps, no pregnant pauses. God had completed three weeks of solid teaching with all of us from early every morning to late into each night. No time had been wasted.

Every single person that was on The Awakening had had miraculous changes in his/her lives, (some of them immediate, some of them coming later,) abundance of all types had manifested in our lives; Love, Peace, Freedom, Financial, Spiritual, Physical, mental and emotional health appeared in all of our lives for the first time. We had also learned that it stays as long as we stay living with God, remaining masters of our inner selves not returning to our old ways; our character defects that had caused us so much pain.

We spent our last night together celebrating with a meal. All the people who had helped with the course came and enjoyed being with us. They had seen miracles happening in front of their eyes, as each of the course members started to change for the better. My Angel and I left them early so that they could continue with their fun. We were exhausted and needed the peace of our own company, and we felt utter relief from finishing the course, proud that we had trusted and seen it through to its end.

Early the next morning all of us, including the English members of the group, decided to go to the airport together to bid our Danish guests a safe journey home. The trip back to the airport was very different from their arrival. Laughter and singing filled the minibus all the way back. Real friendships had been created. Spirits were very high, and everyone was feeling very ebullient with their own achievements.

Living with God

The farewell was emotional. The complete physical, mental, emotional and spiritual exhaustion of everyone was momentarily forgotten, replaced by tears and a real sadness at leaving each other, all mingled with the excitement of going home.

As we drove away leaving the Danish group frantically waving at the kerbside, we felt complete relief and a sense of real achievement. Some of those people had found freedom within themselves for the first time in their lives. What a peaceful drive home we had. Not a word spoken, as each of us was lost in our own personal reflections of this amazing journey.

The Lighthouse was empty again. Four of us now remained for whatever God had in store for us next. One of the English course members had elected to stay on as part of our growing team. She had been shocked and overwhelmed by her invite from Sananda. This was a woman who had never known kindness and unconditional love in her life, and she did not need to be asked twice. The following weeks were peaceful, but our own personal work never ended. We continued with daily lessons with Sananda. We were on a long journey that still is far from over. The mundane issues of life came back to me with a bang.

Chapter 13

The Decree Absolute

The official receiver in charge of the liquidation process of our old company had now elected to put this wonderful building up for auction. A date for its sale had now been set.

The woman I had been married to for 9 years, had been granted a divorce. The decree nisi had been granted shortly after we separated in 2004, and we were awaiting the decree absolute. The reason the divorce had not been finalised was now rearing its head.

We had to decide on the division of our personal assets.

This was my second time at this divorce malarkey. The first time, I had walked away from my ownership of everything material, the home and everything in it. My first wife had thrown me out like a piece of waste paper. I can't blame her. I was a nightmare to live with. I had been a workaholic from a very young age, and I was never there. My children were young and I felt it would be better to leave their home with as little disruption as possible.

However on this occasion, my second divorce, I had not relinquished my ownership in the same way. Under the current system of law in England I was still a 50% owner of the home and all its assets until decreed otherwise by a judge in court. The normal process was to divide everything in half, if there were no dependants in the case. Our children had grown up and left.

This was not how my second ex-wife now saw it. She wanted everything. In the past I had been emotionally lazy. When fights or disputes came, I was prone to let it all go by which I thought was my way of being a good person. The fact is that when I did this, sometime later on I would realise that by just standing by and letting the world have its way with me was creating resentments in me. I had learned that resentments left festering within me were dangerous. They were going to come back to bite me on the arse!

I sought council on this matter.

Come and spend time with me!

I would be very happy to, but what do you mean?

Join me through meditation. We wish you to join us for forty eight hours in silent, fasting meditation!

I had become quite used to sitting in meditation, and I was happy to go along with this. The fasting non-sleeping side of it didn't bother me. I was more concerned about where I was going to pee! Sananda had told me where and how I was to meditate. I was to sit in the centre of the main work room of The Lighthouse surrounded by candles with incense permanently lit throughout the meditation. I was not to leave the room. The Angel and the other two members of our small team could join us throughout the meditation if they wished to. They could come and go in silence as they saw fit.

We made all preparation for this meditation including placing a pot to pee in. It was placed in the corner of the room and at 10.00 am the following morning I entered the meditation. When I had first started the process of meditation some years before, I had struggled to quiet my mind, to sit still and to let go. I thought that it was all garbage.

(What an arsehole I was in the past, and still can be if I let go of the vigilance. I was so opinionated egotistical and judgemental of everything. Full of fear).

Since learning to master some of my character defects I have learned that meditation comes much more easily. I quickly fell into a deep hypnotic state. Over the next 48hours I was taken on a detailed journey of my life, much more detailed than the Christmas carol I spoke of earlier in this book.

I was with Sananda, side by side. Every part of me and my actions, good and bad, were reviewed. Slightly cringing at first I became completely aware of who I had been, who I was now, what my present path was and what the future held. I quickly became aware that no judgements of me were being made in these visions. I was my own judge. I left my body

Living with God

completely just as I had experienced as a child. I was free from all human restraints. Time and distance disappeared.

I travelled the planet moving from one country to another in an instant, I was speeding through the air with images flashing by me so fast that it was humanly impossible to absorb them, and yet I was able to take them all in.

I was being shown things now happening in this world of which I was unaware, things to come and what I should do about some of them.

I was being shown my new path, a path that was to benefit mankind rather than what it was like in the past. The previous person was now gone.

I was starting afresh. I had been given a new name, Raven, a name which I have come to love, a name which I am proud of, a name which stands as a constant reminder of my purpose.

The Raven in Scandinavian mythology is the bird that sits on the shoulders of the God Thor. The Raven is deemed to be the messenger from the Gods.

At 10.00 am 48hours later precisely I came out of the meditation. My Angel was waiting for me eager to hear the news of my journey. I opened my eyes to be greeted by this vision of beauty and love. Overwhelmed by her presence I stood a little shakily after two days of sitting cross legged and hugged her. It felt so good to be alive, free and in deep, deep love with her, with life and with God.

Part of that journey taught me of the need to act differently. Instead of just letting things go I now had to make a stand on the issue of my divorce, contrary to previous guidance I had been given. I was to seek equal justice in the division of assets. The divorce had now moved from the benches of letter writing to a court appearance.

My now nearly second ex-wife had been granted legal aid to secure her case of getting all assets from the marriage. I had been denied such support due to the fact that I was the director of a Ltd. company, even though it was in liquidation. For some reason in this country no one believes you have nothing, if you have held such office in business.

I had to represent myself legally in the whole case. After receiving numerous threatening letters, the day of the court case came.

For the first time in my working life I entered the building without a suit and tie, without briefcase, without the white knuckled apprehension of what was to come.

I was greeted by the barrister and representing council for my ex-wife, a group of tall surly men. They were more likened to what is conjured in the mind at the thought of meeting Mafia representatives. They carried an energy that was threatening, wielding their position of power as legal wizards like slashing sabres.

If I was not going to change my mind right now and give my ex-wife everything, then I would feel the cut of this cold steel. I declined the offer and moved to a seat in the corner of the waiting room.

My ex-wife and her legal council moved off like a rugby scrum into more private quarters to await the call to enter the court room. I felt alone in the courthouse but safe.

My reason for being here was no longer material gain; it was a lesson for me in not just giving in to the slightest oppression. The call came all too soon. My ex-wife and her

Living with God

legal entourage suited and booted ready for war marched into the courtroom ahead of me. I followed in an open neck casual shirt, linen lightweight trousers and flip flops not to be disrespectful in any way, but that was all I owned.

I realised how funny this situation was. In the past this type of situation had frightened the life out of me, people in places of power, like this opposing legal team, would have owned me. Without denying their education I had learned that bullies come in suits as well as scruffs, and that the bullying tactics of such people no longer had power over me.

They could only bully me now if I allowed them to.

Those days were well and truly over. I felt and still feel very sorry for those in society who are still under the powerful influence of bullies; bullies that masquerade under what has been allowed to become acceptable banners of office and where intimidation of the less educated is allowed, in fact promoted.

The courtroom was cold, sparsely furnished with just a table and chairs for each opposing side. The judge sat elevated to the front of the room, dressed in his smart business suit, looking at our arrival over half moon glasses. The legal team opposing me sat down around their table using the spare chairs that I did not need, huddled together like a rugby scrimmage.

The case began with my ex-wife's legal team tearing into me, creating an image of me that I was dishonest, that I was hiding money, other business incomes, property and the like. All of it conjured up in their minds like talented magicians. I nearly believed them myself! I sat quietly while they ripped

Raven

my character apart. All of this was an act to discredit me, and they were well practised in the art of creative fantasy.

There were no factual grounds for my getting less than half of the proceeds of the matrimonial home and contents. They knew it, but relied on their skill of fantastical picture painting to influence the judge against me.

I rebuffed all their allegations as they threw them, but the power of this legal team was wearing me down. My resolve was starting to buckle under the intimidating pressure.

Leave everything and follow me!

What? You told me to come and defend myself, not to allow myself to be walked all over, to see that some justice was served and now you're telling me to leave everything and follow you? I could feel anger rising in me. Are you telling me just to give in to this group of hyenas and buzzards, profiting from the easy pickings of my inability to defend myself as easily as these people are able to discredit me?

Leave everything and follow me. Ask only one question and then give all this materialism to her. Set yourself free of this chain that hangs heavily around your neck, weighing you down with the threat of drawing you into the past behaviour that will only cause you more pain.

Living with God

This message hit me hard right in the middle of this court hearing. I was not sure of why this was happening, but I had learned that my guide Sananda knew better than me. I knew the question I was to ask it appeared in my mind like a neon sign and with it the whole purpose of this charade.

When my daughter Emma had been killed, my nearly second ex-wife, Emma's stepmother the three remaining daughters and I had decided it would be a nice thing for us to remember Emma by choosing to plant a tree in memory of her life from each of us in the grounds of our home. Five trees were selected and we had gone through a ceremony together respectfully planting each tree.

It had been a beautiful process for all of us shortly after her death. The trees represented bright living reminders of Emma that we were able to see from every window and door of our home.

I looked up at the judge from the barrage of verbal venom that was flying at me from the opposition. Their attacks were relentless.

"I do not wish to have anything from the marriage," I spoke softly.

The court room fell silent the hyenas looked at me with broad grins on their faces. They had won.

The judge asked me to repeat what I had said. "I wish for nothing from the matrimonial home or from the proceeds of sale of the matrimonial home or from my nearly ex-wife other than to ask her a question.

Everyone was stunned at the quick change that had happened in the proceedings. The judge granted my request for the question.

I told the story to the court room of the trees we had planted in memory of my dead daughter, and that on my last trip past my property I had noticed that they had all been dug up and Emma's memory in those trees had been destroyed.

"What had happened to them?"

For the first time everyone looked to my ex-wife for an answer. They were all shocked.

Her face crimsoned and fell downwards with her eyes fixed to the floor.

Her legal team recovered from the question quickly barking out loudly to the judge what relevance the question had to the case.

The judge stopped them and asked for the answer.

It really was not necessary to hear the answer, the bitterness, greed, anger and vindictiveness was shown in that moment.

I stood up and thanked the judge for his and the courts time. He quickly ended the case handing everything to my ex-wife. A silent embarrassment hung in the room as the details were quickly noted.

I realised in that moment that this appearance and defence I was making was not the real reason for this hearing. What the hell did I want with old memories of the past wrapped up in material objects that would only remind me of a very painful time in my life, where no love had existed, where hatred and bitterness towards me were the only memories that I would ever get from having any connection to the past.

Living with God

I mentally applauded Sananda for the way in which it had come to its end.

I now felt sorry for this woman in that cold court room. She was now my ex-wife absolute.

I was free while she was stuck in deep pools of emotions that would be with her for the rest of her life, unless she took notice of the gift that God had just given us, the chance to see ourselves as we really are and do something about it.

As always spirit had created an opportunity for change in this process, an opportunity for everyone involved in the case to consider their actions and motives. I walked away from the court house completely free with the best things a man could have as a memory of his daughter, a spiritual connection and happy memories of her life.

I walked back to The Lighthouse, throwing all of the paper connections, letters summons, and evidence of assets into a garbage bin along the route.

This freedom was heaven.

My Angel and Patrick drove to meet me and collected me on the road halfway back from town. They were shocked at my story, yet fully understanding of how and why it had happened. That part of what was my life and all of its attachments had gone. I had now truly let go of everything. Home, family, cars, money, ownership of all material objects from the past were gone.

I stood naked in my freedom like a new born baby, a little scared and yet full of anticipation for the future.

Something else had also gone.

Raven

On a daily basis all that I had been in the past, my character defects had also gone, or, should I say were now safely packed away. My ego, jealousy, manipulation, lying, cheating, envy, anger, control, judgement, opinions, gossip, hatred, bitterness, resentment, selfishness, self pity, deceit, among many other things, were lying dormant, no longer in control of me creating the hell that I had experienced before.

I had turned a corner in my life experience. I no longer wanted to be the creator of my own pain with these negative traits that had haunted my life. Even the tiger that sat at my ear, which I know to be fear, was sleeping peacefully for the moment. All I felt in this moment was love, peace, freedom in magnificent abundance.

Chapter 14

Our last goodbye

The days passed slowly at The Lighthouse as we continued our daily in-tuition with spirit. Any money we had had now ran out. Bills were mounting again, and our small group was starting to see new depths within itself that we had not yet plumbed.

Our food supply was vanishing fast. This place that had once been full of kind, loving, caring and gentle people was now empty but for this small group. No visitors came. No one called. All friends and friendships had gone. Now we were quite alone except for God. One morning came when it all proved too difficult, too great a stretch for two of our group. They had been through enough and decided to leave. It was a very emotional parting. We had been together through so much.

We had become like brothers and sisters. This part of the journey was over. Daily we were being guided to trust by Sananda. We would acquire The Lighthouse for God's work, and all we needed would be provided, but the lack of food, comforts and constant learning tore us apart.

No physical evidence of what we were being told in our spiritual guidance of what was to come was immediately evident.

My Angel and I were alone

What was to happen to us?

Neither of us knew. So far we had trusted God and so far we had been ok Sure it had been tough, but we had also experienced new freedom, peace and love, which in our experience had been more valuable than anything else on the planet.

So often I looked at people in the street rushing from one place to another, cell phone to one ear, a child in another hand dragging it along. Pain etched across their faces with the busyness of life weighing heavily upon them. That was not the life I wanted to live any more.

That was not the way God wanted any of us to live. By coming to know ourselves better through the teachings of Sananda and changing the way we lived, acted and thought, we had moved closer to living with God than ever before. As hard as it was at times, we still preferred what life was now to what life had been in the past.

The car payments on my Angel's little Renault had become overdue again and the pressure of living in our society without the means to support ourselves was starting to stretch me.

One morning I awoke to the sudden realisation that there was no food in the cupboard, no money available anywhere to buy any and even the dog had eaten his last meal with us the previous night.

Living with God

I looked over at my sleeping Angel and the dog lying on the floor beside her. The two of them were completely peaceful. Throughout this whole experience she had not complained once. She was a breath of fresh air to be with.

I looked at her with such admiration and felt the pain of the deepest love for her in my heart. I would then, and still would now, gladly have given my life for her. This Angel had taught me so much, how to value life and what in the past I would have overlooked. She had taught me how to appreciate nature, to see the beauty in simple things, to take the time to really know the world I was living in.

I felt tears well in my eyes as they often did when I took the time to appreciate her in those quiet moments as she slept.

In the past my brain would have been racing to find ways out of this situation. Sometimes some of the ideas would have been not only wrong, but downright dishonest; I had excused myself in the past when converting these ideas into action, telling myself I had no other option. I had to provide for my family.

When I look back now at those times I feel ashamed, I had never been as poor as I was now, but in the past I had done things to continue the level of materialism that my family and I had become used to, and with all the materialism in the world I had never known peace, freedom, happiness and love like I knew it now.

These moments of realisation sobered me and kept my emotions in check; I would have exploded in anger or dissolved into self pity in the past at the thought of my situation. How ugly I had been. The tiger in my ear called fear continued to sleep for a little longer.

I got out of bed, leaving the Angel to sleep, dressed and went to the main workroom of The Lighthouse. I needed to talk with Sananda.

Well, we are completely in your hands now. We have nothing, and I am not resorting to my old ways to change this, so please tell us what we are to do.

I sat on the floor cross legged waiting for an answer, NOTHING CAME.

I had often sat waiting for answers, sometimes never getting them as the teaching I was receiving was in patience, tolerance or some other area that needed practice.

After meditating for sometime I accepted that whatever I was looking for from Sananda that morning was not coming. I spent the day in reflection and hunger looking for the meaning of the lesson.

By the next day I was starting to buckle, I had rationalised that perhaps it was my trust levels that were weak, or my patience that was being tested. Whatever it was, it never altered the fact that I was starting to feel responsible again. Emotions were stirring in me as I realised, but never accepted my powerlessness over our predicament.

The sleeping tiger in my ear awoke and started to whisper. Negativity engulfed me.

I realised that I was out of control again.

Anger swept over me as I shouted at God. Why are you **fucking** with me?

I have done everything you have asked of me, and this is how you treat me! The bailiffs are coming again, the

Living with God

car is being repossessed, The Lighthouse is being sold from underneath us, and we are helpless about it. No food, no friends, no family, no money, no transport, no nothing!

All these promises you have given me, none of them are coming true.

Not even the Angel you promised would come to help with the course appeared. AAAAAAAAAAARRRRRRHHHHHH HHHHHHHHHHHHHHHHH!

I screamed as loud as I could. I threw myself around the room like a child in a wild tantrum; I thrashed, kicked and screamed until I was spent. I crumpled sobbing on the floor. In that moment I had seen how much faith I had.

I walked back to the little cottage in the grounds of The Lighthouse exhausted. My Angel and my dog, Finnegan, what was to happen to them? Two days without food?

I spent the rest of the morning in silence. I had explained to my Angel what had happened that morning. In silence she smiled at me. Her eyes locked with mine full of the deepest love. Have faith Raven. God will look after us.

Two hours later a knock came on the cottage door. I answered it and standing in front of me was a man in his seventies, rotund with a long white beard and a big smile on his face. In his hand he carried a large carrier bag.

He introduced himself as Philip. He was the husband of the woman who had come to the course with her team of women to provide massages and reflexology for the course we had run earlier in the year.

Here is the angel I sent you. Receive openly what he has to give you and know that we have never forsaken you.

I invited Phillip in, and he walked in like Father Christmas with his sack of presents. he had heard of our plight, believed in the work we were doing to help others and decided to help us.

In the carrier bag were items of food for the Angel and I that he had taken from his own shelves and freezer. At the bottom of the bag were two large tins of dog food.

In that moment I felt more humble than ever before, this was an angel.

Thank you God. I am sorry for doubting you!

We sat and talked together for a long time, listening to Finnegan tucking into his succulent bowl of dog food. I swear I realised a pleasure from that experience that was immeasurable.

Phillip told us of his life and experience, of his triumphs and failings without reserve.

We became instant friends, understanding each other, feeling like family that had never met before.

To have someone outside ourselves that believed in us and our goals was worth more than the much needed food.

Phillip came back to us regularly with food supplies taken from his own home. He and his wife were hardly able to afford their own needs let alone taking care of ours, but their determination to help in this way was truly a gift from God.

The weeks went by without much change except that the pressure of our debts was building as the sale of The Lighthouse loomed ever closer.

Daily we were being visited by prospective purchasers; families, couples and property developers. It was hard to consider that The Lighthouse was going to become something other than a place of healing.

One morning I was visited by The Good Doctor and his partner. They had come to take the remaining items from the building that had been part of the previous company we had owned together. The visit was strained. Our friendship had gone. All belief in what we were doing and representing was over.

He asked me to ensure him that I would leave the property on completion of the sale, and of where would we go. I told him that of course we would leave after the sale, but where we would go to we did not know. I sensed his disinterest in our future. After all, why should he be interested in us? his need was to sell the property, and I understood this clearly.

As he and his partner left the property with a loaded van, I felt a deep sadness within me. We had been such good, close friends for such a long time. We had battled against systems that were penal to man and succeeded, if only for a short time. We had stood shoulder to shoulder as warriors, and now it was all over. I never saw them again. What I do know is that these two people had given their lives, money, home and everything that they were to creating a difference, and they had achieved it. I will always admire them for their courage. What they did still makes a difference today.

The Lighthouse was sold on the day of the auction for a loss of £225,000.00 to the company and the company, was wound up; finished.

The Good Doctor, his partner and I lost any hope of getting back our own financial investment.

The sale of the building was the letting go of the final part of my past. It was the only thing that held me tied to the person I had been.

The Angel, Finnegan and I stayed in the building for the next few weeks while the legal transactions of the sale were taking place.

What has happened to your guidance that we would purchase the Lighthouse?

You have!

Call me stupid or what, but it has been sold to someone else.

The Lighthouse that we have spoken of is within you. Your body is the house and the light of God is what shines within you. You have paid the price for acquiring it with your faith, self work and diligence. Wherever you go The Lighthouse goes with you. Wherever you are The Lighthouse that you have become will give warm loving care to those who need it. The Lighthouse

Living with God

that you are becoming is far greater than the bricks and mortar of a building, for in you lies the evidence that God is, and all who come to you shall know it. Living with God is open to all who that seek it, as you have, and to all those who seek it, so shall they find us waiting.

That is a powerful statement. What if I fall and God leaves me?

We will never leave you! It is only you that can leave us, and should your Lighthouse crumble, you can rebuild it again time after time. Keep the lessons that you have learned throughout this journey as the guidelines for living with God, and the mortar between the bricks of your house will stay firm. No canon will breach them, no fire will destroy them. The walls will grow larger and larger, giving room for more people to enter and know you, to see that what shines in you, shines in them also.

I laughed and the Angel laughed. I have learned that things can be very different from what I expect, and that to expect is to be open to disappointment. I had learned that the unexpected is what happens when living with God, and that can be a lot of fun. I have learned that the tiger of fear stays asleep in my ear all the time when I accept that God is in control.

For some strange reason I felt no fear. We were only days away from getting out of The Lighthouse and still we had nowhere to go. We had no money to rent a home and no offers from anyone of somewhere to stay. I had visited the local authorities to try and obtain accommodation without success.

They advised me to stay in the building until we were officially evicted through the normal processes of law. Then the authorities would be obliged to accommodate my Angel and myself. The dog would have to go! Eviction was inevitable, but this way at least a bed would be provided for us, so I would be keeping my word of leaving when the property was sold. It just created a minor delay.

We waited quietly for the court order to arrive and it did. I paid my last visit to the courthouse on the day of the eviction hearing. Sitting in the familiar waiting room was surreal. I felt very happy, peaceful and full of love.

To the onlooker that knew of my circumstances I would have appeared quite insane. A lawyer from London had come to represent the opposition that wished to have me evicted, a tall slim elegant black woman.

As she approached me I saw her armour build around her ready for a fight. With each step towards me she grew harder and harder. I noted how much we have to fight against our natural selves in order to become what society has forced us to become, harsh and unforgiving beings.

Living with God

Before she got to me, I felt sorry for her, seeing the pain of who she had become in that short walk. So distant from the person she truly was, a warm, gentle, loving woman. I held out my hand to her with a big smile on my face which shocked her. Her life in the work place was full of ugly confrontation and hurt. To be greeted in this way took the wind out of her sails.

For a split second she melted, held firmly in my eyes, speechless. Her head was telling her one thing, her heart telling her another. She quickly recovered her composure and spouted through unsure lips her intent to get me out of the house quickly and painfully, if I objected to her seeking eviction today. I looked deeply into her eyes not flinching, and thanked her for her guidance and for travelling all this way to see me.

She was disarmed. Turning on her heel with a click of her mouth she stomped away to await the call to the hearing.

This was fun. Feeling no fear, but accepting that whatever the outcome was to be would be God's will. I was enjoying this freedom.

The call from the court usher came. She called my name and the opposing solicitor's name out loud in the open waiting room which was full of people. In the past I would have been mortified at this. I would not have wanted anyone to know I was there. So great was my ego.

My name being shouted in a public place, what a humiliation. All eyes looked at me as I stood to enter the courtroom; I noticed that this was the first time that I felt no humiliation or ego in such a situation. I smiled at all the waiting people and walked off behind the strutting opposition lawyer.

As we entered the judge's room a warm smile came over the judge's face. He knew me well, and he knew why I was here today. He had seen me through most of my downfalls (as society would see it), but which in fact were not downfalls, but a rising of a free spirit. He acknowledged me, and I felt an almost fatherly protection in his smile.

It was like the final execution for him. After this it was all over, and he seemed to have a certain respect for me. It did not take long. In the judge's summing up, after giving the eviction the "Go ahead", he had no choice; He looked to me and said,

"Well, at least it is all over. I hope that you find some peace after all this."

The opposing lawyer looked at me with triumph on her face, and I smiled at her holding her eyes locked tight. She was unable to look away. I knew that in that moment she felt something change within her. Although the law and lawyers are necessary, I knew that compassion and kindness would play a bigger part in her attitude towards people in the future. It did not have to be a war.

I left the courthouse for the last time. I now knew the date we had to leave our precious Lighthouse.

The days ticked away quickly towards getting out of the building still with nowhere to go. Please tell me what we are to do?

For some time now we had been living on food parcels gifts from our new angel Phillip, Things were exactly as spirit had told me they would be. We had everything we needed

Living with God

to survive for each day. I had finally accepted that when living with God everything is perfect and often right at the last minute, whatever is needed by me is provided. I had learned to let go of the control around my future. All fear had gone.

Beloved Raven. You are now living with God. Have no fear and we will guide your every move. Listen carefully and follow. Connect with Lars in Denmark. Offer yourselves to move to his country and work. Take The Lighthouse to these people; they are in need of your service. We will provide you with everything. Go to Salisbury to the garage on the main road. There is a gift there for you from God. It will carry you to your destination.

I told the Angel of this message from Sananda. Feeling very excited at this news we jumped into my Angels Renault and drove off into town. Crazy! Really we never even had money to put petrol in our car, and we were going to a garage.

As we approached the garage we saw it, magnificent standing on the garage forecourt like a beacon calling to us. Everything else seemed to fog. All we could see as we drove up to the garage was this magnificent white Chevrolet Tahoe. An American left hand drive 4x4.

("It seems silly to call it that as it is more like a space ship than a 4x4")

Raven

The vehicle had been customised with large chromium wheels, and it had an LPG conversion so that it ran on dual fuel. Our breaths were taken away.

This was not a car you ever saw in England. It was far too big for our roads, an engine size that would mean it was financially unviable to run without the LPG conversion. We stopped at the garage, and the Angel and I got out of our small car and stood staring at the Chevy. There were many other English 4x4's standing beside it, but this one stood out.

This is for you! Accept this gift from God!

I was done with arguing and asking how and why. If this was a fantasy then just for this moment we enjoyed this opulence, even if it was a dream. The owner of the garage saw us admiring the vehicle and quickly came towards us. He was a tall slim man. I could see him changing physically in front of me as he strode towards us putting on his invisible salesman's uniform, getting his book of mental sales techniques prepared for whatever he had to say in order to get a sale. It was like watching a film. This salesman like all other people had had to become something totally different from his real self in order to do his job. I remember thinking then how sad it is that none of us are good enough as we are. Society has created a model into which we all have to fit into in order to be acceptable.

I felt the realisation of our financial position hitting me like a meteor. I could not lie to this man and pretend that I wanted to purchase his vehicle.

> *Then do not lie! Enjoy this gift and tell him you wish to purchase it. Try it out. Believe in us and we will not forsake you.*

The owner of the garage enthused over this rarity that he had for sale and showed us every detail of the car. It was sheer luxury. He pointed out the clever little gadget that sat in the dash, and he said it was designed to tell me when police were in the area.

(I later learned that it was actually a device for telling you how much space was behind you when reversing).

Our little dog, who had now turned into a big lovable Boxer, could no longer fit into the back of our little Renault and complained bitterly when we squeezed him into it. He would have space in the rear luggage compartment that was so big he could run around in it if he wanted. We helped him up into this new luxurious space and laughed as we looked at him unsure of what was going on. He was looking around him at all this space, scared. This highlighted to me how we would all rather stay in our small space. Even though it is cramped at least we know it. We stay in it rather than step into the unknown.

After a short time and now steeled with our reassurance he stretched out enjoying this new found freedom. His look of "Is this really for me? Are you sure?" will stay with me forever. Our dog, Finnegan, had shown us so much love and given us so much comfort when everything else seemed so dark.

Raven

After a test drive my Angel and I connected visually, nodding our delight to each other. We did not have to ask each other. We just knew that this was from God. I was unable to stop my mouth from uttering the words, "We would like to purchase it."

I was frozen to the spot as the words fell out of my mouth, God knew I was scared and so took over my words and actions.

The garage owner rubbed his hands with glee. This would not have sold easily under normal circumstances. Who would want such a car which was designed for driving on the opposite side of the road and would guzzle fuel like there was no tomorrow?

He did not hang around. We told him of the situation of overdue payments on the Renault, and together we sat and discussed how it could all be resolved.

We finally drove away from the garage with the knowledge that in order for us to settle the debt on the Renault and purchase the Chevrolet Tahoe in cash, we needed £12,000.00. Like insane children we drove away from the garage laughing. We had to laugh, we never had a pot to piss in, and we were looking at spending all this money on a new car.

In that moment, "Big Bertha", the cars new name came to me. While we had been to see the Big Bertha, we had advised the garage owner of our situation and asked him to find us a Hire Purchase company that would lend us the money. My credit rating was appalling and I stood no hope of getting finance. It was down to my Angel.

When we arrived back at our home, which would no longer be in a week, I quickly went to the telephone and

Living with God

called Lars in Denmark to continue with my instructions from Sananda. Lars was one of the people who had been to The Awakening in January of that year. He and his family had experienced dramatic positive life changes since the course. I told him that we were guided to come to Denmark to offer our services to those who needed them and that we would very much like to work with him.

He was bowled over by this and asked to call us back later. I agreed and set a time for the call. My Angel and I sat waiting for the call. We had packed most of our belongings and arranged for a removals company to collect our few items of furniture on the morning of our eviction.

We had no idea what was going to happen to us. What we did know, was that we were powerless over our situation. We had tried to take care of ourselves, but everything had seemed against our staying in England.

When I had tried to get the authorities to re-house us it meant loosing our dog and living in one room of a house, sharing the remaining space with other people. Sharing did not bother us, but loosing Finnegan was not going to happen.

We owed him too much for the unconditional love he had given us. We were prepared to move into the canvas tent we had, if necessary. The garage owner called us frequently with the advice that no one was interested in lending us the money to purchase Big Bertha and settle our existing debt on the little Renault which was so close to repossession. Our hearts sank momentarily.

The call finally came from Lars. His family and the good people of Denmark that we had come to know from working

Raven

with them, were all excited at the prospect of our going to live and work there.

Together they had worked out everything about how this could be done. We were offered a caravan in which to live and more than enough work to do.

Since the miracles of "The Awakening" other people had heard of and witnessed the profound changes that had happened to the small group of people that had come to The Lighthouse and asked God for help. They were queuing up to see us and book appointments with us. We would be able to extract ourselves from our financial difficulty very quickly. Within three days the exact amount of money, to the penny, that was needed to purchase Big Bertha, settle our debts and travel to our new home, arrived in our bank. This was incredible. We were slowly becoming used to the miraculous happening around us.

We thank you, God.

My Angel and I could not contain our excitement. We thanked God a lot. Choosing to live with God was the best thing we had ever done not because of the car or the lessons or anything else, but the love we shared together; it was getting deeper and deeper and a lot more fun.

It over-spills from our cup to fill the cups of all those who came near us. This love is not ours. It is God's, and it flows in such abundance that all who choose to can share it. The joy we have both been privileged to witness at seeing this love impact on other human beings is infectious.

Giving of ourselves has become our life blood. By connecting with other people in the spirit of love, the

Living with God

more we give the greater our love experience becomes. It's wild!!

My Angel, Finnegan and I drove to the garage to collect Big Bertha. No one was more surprised than the garage owner when we arrived. With a huge smile on our faces we handed him a very dodgy looking debit card that had not seen the light of day for a very long time. He looked at us both bemused and questioning. Are you paying a deposit?

"No, we replied."

Take the full payment for the settlement of the purchase and the debt on the little Renault.

He was flabbergasted.

He said, "I don't know how you have done this, but I am bloody amazed". He had warmed to us in our previous meetings, at the honesty when telling him of our situation, and at the love that he experienced when in our company.

He ran the debit card through his machine, tapping in the total amount for the settlement, fully expecting it to be declined. As the little machine whirred and clicked, he watched in silence. Ding!

The approval code came through for the amount of money requested. It had now been transferred to his bank. My Angel and I just watched him. It was so much fun to do this. His eyebrows rose in stunned silence at the approval, and he just gazed at the little approval docket for a few moments.

"I am amazed! Bloody amazed! Have you robbed a bank?"

"No, we have just trusted in our beliefs and this is what happens."

He did not care how we had done it. We felt his real pleasure at our getting Bertha. No longer was his pleasure held in his selling it. He was engulfed with the love that came from us, and he was sharing our joy.

I had felt from the judge in the courthouse on my final visit that feeling of fatherly protection. Here it was again coupled with a sincere happiness at our success in achieving our goals.

We drove our gift from God home laughing like crazy kids. It was like a dream, something created out of a fantasy world which exists only in the mind. But this was for real.

The day of leaving came all to soon. The removal company arrived at 7.00 am to get our things out quickly. We had told them that we were being evicted and that the gates to the premises would be chained at 8.30 am by the bailiff and who would also change all of the door locks.

It has been a wonderful experience to feel the warmth that comes from people when they learn the truth of what is happening: the judge, the garage owner and now the removal men were giving off that now familiar energy of fatherly protection towards us.

When I asked them how and when they wished to be paid, they simply said not to worry, that they would take care of our things until we needed them and not to worry about paying them yet. Things would change for us.

They felt it.

It took them only 40 minutes to empty our little cottage: a bed, fridge and settee were the only large items to go. We quickly finished cleaning and mopping the empty shell. The removal men left, and we were standing in the building together holding hands in silence. We were feeling the whole experience of what we had done here. All of the things that had happened raced through our minds like a rolling film being played back to remind us.

This had been our haven, our school, and most of all this was the place where we and so many others had found freedom, peace and love.

We left the cottage, handing the keys to an empty building into the eager hands of the waiting receiver. The whole property was now empty; just another large country house and a small cottage. We said our last goodbye.

The Lighthouse continued out of the gates represented now by our bodies as we drove away to our new beginning in Denmark. All sadness left as we drove away. We realised what God had meant in so many of our lessons.

The only thing of value in life is love. The only thing that is real in life is love. It is who we are, what we are and where we will all go back to, as love is the source of our beginnings. it is where we all come from.

Chapter 15

The unknown

My Angel, Finnegan and I drove for two days, leaving England without any regrets, driving into the unknown, into an unfeared future. Late in the evening of the second day we arrived in Denmark. In total darkness we were trying to find a little caravan on a cold night in the middle of the Danish countryside after going down many wrong roads. We finally found the right one and we were met at the caravan by Nina, the sister of Lars. Nina was a young lady who had spent many months with us in the Lighthouse. It was a pleasure to be met by a happy smiling face of someone who was genuinely pleased to see us. Nina was one of the first people who we had worked with since the changes in ourselves had started to take place. She had locked herself away from life in isolation and solitude. Inside her own mind was the only place that she had been able to find the comfort that she needed, away from the harsh realities of life that had been very punishing to her. She was a very attractive young woman who had not seen her own beauty for many years. Now all of that was in the past. She too had found freedom by working with herself and following the guidance received through our bodies from spirit. It was such a joy for us to see this new woman that greeted us now.

Denmark reminded me of the country that I had called home and grown up in: green and wet, a country where I had served in the armed forces on active duty; a country to which I no longer felt attached. Like so many things in my old life it was gone. I was now a citizen of the world, free to go wherever God sent me, wherever I could be of service in love to others.

The caravan was small, about twelve feet long but very well appointed, It could sleep two and a dog comfortably. Nina left us to settle in shortly after our arrival. After she had gone my Angel and I looked at each other for signs of disapproval without uttering a word. It ended with a smile and a big hug as we both welcomed each other to our new home.

We spent the next two weeks getting to know our surroundings. The caravan was parked next to a fjord, and every morning we would walk or cycle along the paths next to it. Finnegan settled quickly into a new routine, racing round the Danish countryside. We were all very happy and enjoyed the space, away from all of the problems of the past, free to enjoy each other's company and explore more of who we were.

The rest of the world disappeared for those two weeks. My Angel and I loved each other without reserve, exploring the depths of our emotions and bodies. We had been together through some very difficult times, and now we were free to enjoy ourselves. No bailiffs or unpleasant callers to disturb us, no fears that so often in the past had occupied our minds drawing us away from the love.

I had known lust in the past and the excitement of a new relationship, that excitement had soon worn off and the mundane reality of life had taken over. That was my experience.

Some people call those early days of a relationship the honeymoon period. I knew it well and had accepted it like so many of us do. Many of us are Living a life that is far from what God wishes for us, and yet we accept it.

I have seen so many people just existing within a so called marriage or long term relationship in pain hurting each other all because someone or something said they had to. After all I had spent 24 years of my life in two such relationships. A young lady asked me not so long ago how I could be giving people advice on relationships when all I had to show for twenty four years was two failed marriages.

In one sense she was right. I certainly could not advise people on how to have a good relationship, but I could tell them how to screw one up, and if they did not do what I had done, they stood a better chance of creating something lasting.

The truth is, I had never known love or what love is in any way other than the love I had felt for my daughters. That was a pure love that came from within me not born of lust. Other than that, my life had been void of love, and I had craved it so much. It has only been since giving up my will and seeking God's that I have started to learn what love truly is.

What I was now experiencing was that thrill of the new relationship; this new relationship with my Angel had started two years ago and was getting better and better. In the past the lust in any other relationship for me would have vanished by now. My Angel and I could not bear to be away from each other for a moment. Our hearts pined for each other. We talked endlessly, sometimes all day and night, stopping only to dive into the passionate embrace of making love.

I caressed every tiny golden hair that covered her body, feeling the electricity of each strand as our two energies connected, feeling the passion rising and falling in both of us. Our breathing became as one as we traversed the heavens; our bodies locked in glorious spasms. Hours disappeared as we revelled in the ecstasy of physical orgasm after orgasm. We celebrated our spiritual beings in physical love.

My Angel taught me how to love in every sense of the word; I was and still am a very attentive student.

I discovered that practicing peace, love, freedom and honesty in all areas of my life was not as easy as it sounds, but it's a price well worth paying. I also discovered how distorted from our true selves we become in order to fit in with society and its rules.

After two weeks our Danish hosts started to seek us out. We had been left to our own devices for long enough as far as they were concerned, and our reason for being here started to take shape.

Work came from all directions. People with every kind of illness and dysfunction in their lives were appearing as if by magic. We started to teach them what we had learned. As always for some it was readily accepted and put into practice with phenomenal results. Others they wanted a magic cure, a pill or a promise that relieved them from taking responsibility for themselves. For those people our guidance failed.

We were subjected to praise and ridicule by these two opposite groups and learned to accept that this is God's world, and the type of people in it would only change their lives, if they were prepared to face themselves.

We quickly gave up trying to save everyone. We learned that it is only when people have truly had enough of the way things are in their life, only then are they likely to change.

We learned that you cannot want for other people what they do not want enough for themselves. So many mothers and fathers wanted their offspring to become well through our guidance, but were not prepared to look at themselves to find the cause of the illness in their child in the first place. To heal the child, the source of the problem had to be removed or changed first.

We saw over and over that relationships were the cause of the dis-ease. So many of us have sought to blame others for our misfortune and difficulty and that applies to every area of our lives.

For the first time in a very long time we started to earn income and feel the benefit of eating good food. We only ate organic, avoiding sugar and alcohol. We had discovered that eating fast food, rubbish and giving the body crutches like alcohol and drugs of all kinds was a thing that we only wanted to do when we were under some emotional challenge. We learned that facing the challenge would result in far less damage happening to our bodies, and the need for all of the

Living with God

crutches was gone from us. We taught the same to those who came to us with amazing results.

Living in a caravan was a good experience for me; I had spent too many years living high on the hog.

Fancy hotels and restaurants, fast cars and a lavish lifestyle had taken its toll on me. A massively inflated ego had become one of my heavy crosses. Now I was learning to wash quickly in a cold damp public toilet block, empty the toilet pot and carry water, as well as cleaning the sewage disposal area of the decaying faeces that were left by uncaring people each day, and I was enjoying it. It helped to clear out any remnants of that major ego which I had once followed. I was a different man, happy to live with what God gave me, rather than with the continuous struggle to get more and have more. That needing to have more had been self-imposed in order to satisfy my feeling of worth.

I felt as worthy as any other man all due to my choice to live with God.

The autumn months went by taking us into winter. The cold Scandinavian winds came freezing everything, followed by snowstorms that left snowdrifts piled high enough for us to have to dig ourselves out. We heated ice to melt it for drinking.

One week before Christmas God gave us another gift. We were offered four rooms to rent in a very old farmhouse in the north of the island, with an indoor shower. We were in seventh heaven. Taking no time to accept this offer of a larger space to live in, we quickly set about decorating and cleaning the rooms that had been inhabitable, and within days we were ready with our few belongings to move in. It was a good Christmas. My life had become magical.

January saw more and more work coming to us. I spent days in service as Sananda spoke through my body to countless people; Sananda created, directed and taught courses that changed people's lives. I was just the messenger, not knowing what was to take place at any given time. I just turned up and God did the work. Since I had let go of all control and got out of the way, things just flowed. People got better in every way.

My Angel and I found that the energy that worked with and through us became so powerful that people broke down in tears as they entered our space. Without being asked, they started to cough up emotional blockages, like phlegm which poured out of them in verbal torrents, to be left spent and exhausted, yet free and feeling physically lighter. We found that people needed to connect with God in the form of spirit, Sananda, Allah, Buddha, Red Feather, White Eagle, the angels, call it what you like, they are all of the same energy. It was so strong that we became engulfed by these spiritual hunters, people who had such a thirst for connection to God differently from what they had experienced.

Society is not giving man what man needs. An enormous hole has grown in the fabric of religion which has been created by man, and people are either falling through it or running away from it at a fast rate of knots in a desperate search to find a connection to God to fill their spiritual void that is getting worse.

All connection with England had ceased for us. It was as though we had never existed there. I had let go of everything that I owned. Because of my changes every friendship I had known had ceased some because they did not like what I had become, and others just because those relationships had come to the end of their journey and had died with the old me.

I realised that these relationships were only surface ones and really had no depth to them. What I needed now was honest, deep relationships. I could no longer live in the façade that my past had been.

I no longer wore the mask that I had created to hide behind. The pleasure that I feel from being comfortable in my own skin, accepting myself, warts and all, is immeasurable. This was the freedom that I had been promised by God. It had meant leaving everything and everyone I knew behind, but it was so worth it.

My Angel and I had been guided to create a formal business out of what we were doing in Denmark with Lars, our friend, as a business partner. Lars is one of those reliable methodical men, who just make sure that everything is done properly when it needs to. He provides the physical logistical support that is needed to make the wheels of any business run smoothly.

The business grew and grew. We had gone from nothing to what was becoming a sizeable company in a very short space of time. Our lives were continuously changing with the level of work we were exposed to and the ongoing in-tuition that we were receiving from our spiritual guides.

It was as if we had been put on to a fast track of learning, which was fantastic but exhausting. We came to see the world we lived in with new eyes. I can only describe it this way. It was opening a new book full of pictures.

We were able to see things in people that would not have been seen before, read their thoughts (which I must admit freaked out some of our clients) and feel the truth in their statements far deeper than ever we had before.

We were constantly being shown the bigger picture of what was happening with people and their journeys. We became aware of the enormous impact that energy plays in human life. After all we are all energy, and over periods of years we shut down to our sensitivity to these energies and become stuck in a three dimensional goldfish bowl.

Speech is a very human form of communication, quite cumbersome in its abilities to express thoughts, feelings and emotions compared to energy. We have found the vocabulary of energy to be considerably wider and have learned to communicate with people on an energetic level, talking to the subconscious, implanting new information that helps the person to heal, to break free of the dis-ease that they suffer.

Human eyes have such an important role in human communication. The old saying that the eyes are the window to the soul is so true. I have learned to speak to the souls of people now and not just to the whimsical conscious mind that ducks and dives, weaves and bobs, like a boxer trying to avoid the next punch, driven by fear.

The soul speaks the truth, and is not afraid to ask for what it needs. It allows itself to connect with the Source. The Source is that substance from which we all come before physical birth and to where we will all eventually go back.

Living with God

It is an energy force stronger than anything man can create. It is the energy of love, and it is universal. We come into human life to experience a different dimension of the Source (love).

The Source is God and we are all a part of it.

I have found that every human being is on the same journey, the journey back to this source, and we are all able to help each other fulfil our journeys by giving of ourselves unconditionally. When we do so we become a conduit for the Source (love), to flow through us, giving the vital medicine that we all need to heal. When the soul is healed, then so can the physical, mental and emotional form heal.

The months passed. Our journey was becoming evermore interesting.

I was privileged to work with Sananda, one of the greatest teachers ever to walk this planet. Whenever I sat to channel this energy, I knew I would be able to take the opportunity of learning whatever was being taught, and when I feel the energy of Sananda enter my body, it is like a cloud that engulfs me, filling me with the most incredible feelings of peace. I feel myself being moved over to one side like a spectator within my own body, as Sananda takes over the driving seat.

It is time for you to leave. Our work here is done for the time being.

This message came out of the blue. I was fully immersed in our day to day work, and it hit me with a jolt.

Raven

Ok, what are we to do?

Raven you are to leave this country by the 5th of June. Hand over the work here to Lars and his partner and go back to England. Lars and his partner have called forth this time of teaching and learning for themselves. We have planted the seeds of change in all who we have worked with here. They are deeply sown and they will grow. It is now up to the farmers who have allowed these seeds to be planted in the soil of their beings to tend them.

It was only five days before the 5th of June. Talk about change.

Unexpected ? no! We just accepted.

The following day we went to see Lars and his partner to tell them of our news and the guidance we had received. We told them that we would leave by the Friday of the following week and asked if they were prepared to take over the business that we had created together.

A mixture of excitement and fear burst through their bodies. They had been talking of creating a healing centre and working with people, learning more of the things that they had experienced through us. Little did they know how quickly their pillow talk was to become something more than dreams God was listening. We left them after several hours to assimilate what had been presented and figure out what they wanted and how they would complete everything and take over the business by Friday of the following week.

My Angel and I drove home. We were bemused by this sudden change of events. What was in store for us now? God knew! We had learned to follow.

Within the next five days we packed up our few belongings again. Lars and his partner came to see us on Thursday evening. They had accomplished all that was needed to take over the company, and we could leave the next day. We spent many hours talking. Fear had become a bigger part of their daily life since this decision had been made.

We understood that it was one thing to dream of a wonderful Utopia but another to have the courage to follow the dreams into reality and conquer all the risks that it contained, trust and commitment, to name just two of the emotions that were now screaming inside them.

We admired their courage to face themselves and show each other that they were prepared to commit to each other in ways that would bind them together for the future.

We learned that God is incredibly clever. There are always multiple reasons for things happening in our lives. The events of our lives create ripples that impact in other people's lives without our knowing, and these ripples can create wonderful opportunities which are sometimes stormy. It is only when we accept that after every storm there is an incredible peace that brings new beginnings, that the storms can become welcome guests in our lives.

Friday came all too quickly. Everything was packed and ready to go,

Where?

All we knew was England. We handed back to the farmer the four rooms that he had allowed us to rent from him. He was very happy at the improved condition in which they were left. A small group of people we had become very close to, had come to wish us well on the next part of our journey. A sombre mood hung over them. We had become an integral part of their lives, as they all had become in ours. It was now changing. For some it created fear and for others freedom. We knew that for them and for us to continue on our life journeys, the Angel and I had to get out of the way. We hugged them all and left. My Angel, Finnegan and I felt emotional and yet very peaceful as we drove the three hours to the ferry that would transport us out of Denmark and into Germany that night.

Two more days of driving brought us back to Dover. It felt strange to be back. This country was familiar, but no longer held the emotions of home for us. We knew then and now that our current stay is only temporary.

We spent the next fourteen days in hotels. We had been guided by Sananda to visit all the places in which we had lived and worked previously, all the places that had been part of our journeys; some of them very painful. We noticed the change in ourselves as we drove around. These places still held a part of us. The energy attachment of our past still clung to us like limpets sending shivers of memory through our bodies. We severed our link to each one of them with a Shamanic ceremony. The feeling was amazing as we more and more let go.

We finished this clearance of the past links completely exhausted, and checked into a hotel in Salisbury. By now even the dog just wanted to stay somewhere a little more permanent.

After a meal in our room my Angel fell asleep on the bed with Finnegan. I sat and watched them for a long time.

My family now lay sleeping peacefully in front of me. My heart began to cry. I was so in love with this angel who had accepted me for who and what I am, had loved me like no other when I had nothing, and the little dog who had become so important as a teacher to me. I had learned to acknowledge my heart. Ignoring it in the past had cost me dearly. I mirrored the emotion in my heart as I felt the tears gently streaming down my face. In my mind I thought, if I died right now, I would not be sad. What I have experienced with these two beautiful creatures is the wonder of living with God. I have truly known love.

It is time to begin the next part of our journey. You are to go to Wales, and there is a home there for you all to rest in. It is God's house. It will be the beginning of learning to live with self in ways that you have not yet known, to find a deeper understanding of what it means to live with God! In this place we will write our first book together. This book, the first of many, will be a blueprint for others to learn a new way of life, a life that gives them the opportunity to learn a new freedom, peace and love. They too can share in this, when they put into action what is needed to come closer to God!

I accessed the internet in the late hours of the night while my Angel and Finnegan slept. Sananda guided me to the website that I needed and immediately the home we are now living in came up on the screen, the first and only house I looked at.

This is our gift to you. Take comfort here and with our love know that we are always with you. Our light shines in all those who seek God!

A little stunned at what I was being shown, I sat back for a moment. Was this for real? This place you are showing me is beyond any luxury I have ever known. Is this not just becoming part of my extravagant past again, a past that has hurt me so much.

Allow the abundance that God wishes for you to manifest in your life. This is only the beginning. Our love for you is greater than all the material wealth in your world, and it is this love that is our greatest gift to you.

What can I say? For someone who had never known love, here I am surrounded in a greater abundance of it than words can express. It had taken forty two years of my life to learn that I was not happy, another six years to let go of my past and the person I had become., (Now with the lessons described in the back of this book it has taken a year to put them into action and start receiving the grace and abundance of God.

Thank you, God!

I slept like a baby that night, soundly next to my family, very happy.

Over breakfast the next morning I told my Angel of the previous night's discussions with Sananda. I could see the relief appear on her face. She was tired, but had never complained once; accepting whatever God's will was for us. We quickly drove to Wales. The property that Sananda had shown me was waiting for us. With the money God had given us from our time working in Denmark, God helped us secure this wonderful home to live in for the next six months or until Sananda would tell us differently.

I could never have imagined what twists and turns my life could hold and how much it could change for the better in the space of time we have written about. How much God wants for me and you is beyond our comprehension. I am learning that by giving God the reigns of my life, God has created something I could never have dreamed of experiencing.

I strongly recommend it to those that are searching for what I am now experiencing. "I now know Freedom, Peace and Love".

Living here and feeling what it is like to live with God is beyond simple explanation for me, and I guess that will be in the next book as I spend each day in-tuition. What I do know is that living with God is simple, not complex and difficult, and I have used simple language in detailing some of the recent events of my life in this book, as it is only simple language that I understand. I am sure it may help some of you to find what I have.

I have written the guidelines that I have been given for living with God on the ongoing pages of this book and some of the wonderful teachings that I have received and recorded daily from the exquisite experience that I have been fortunate to undergo. Every time I look at these guidelines, I am constantly reminded of my journey so far, and I try to remember to incorporate these powerful messages into my daily living. If things start to go pear shaped for any reason, the guidelines quickly show me where I am beginning to buckle, and I can straighten myself out quickly. In the space of one year I have gone from riches to rags, from emotional stagnation to complete fulfilment, from being alone to being alive, from being loveless to completely loving and being loved. My personal and domestic circumstances have become better than they ever were all because I hand my life and my will to God every day. His/her choices for me are incredible, and as long as I stay on track, I am sure this abundance will continue to flow.

Sananda, I just want to ask you one other thing before we close this chapter.

Then ask

What's next?

Live each and every moment as though it was your last. Enjoy all the abundance that we bring to you. Demonstrate in your being the power of living with God. Through your demonstration of living life you will attract others who wish to find what you have found.

Thank you.

Lessons from Living with God

Take these lessons and learn them well, for they are the keys to our kingdom. In living these lessons you live with God. As God and in God's image you will demonstrate the existence of eternal life in heaven.

Judgement

No man has the right to judge another. The right of judgement lies only with God. It is with God that man will see who and what he is. Whatever another man does to you or to others does not qualify you to be either judge or jury. By judging others you are only judging yourself. It leads to inflated ego and resentment, the poison that brings about your own downfall through the creation of a spiritual void.

Manipulation

So much abuse of others is created through the terrible dis-ease of destructive manipulation. Those who manipulate others for their own gain will ultimately suffer. However, every communication is a manipulation of sorts. Take care to be sure that what you communicate, therefore manipulate, is for the better good of all concerned. No man has the right to control another for his own good; doing so destroys his soul and weakens the essence of those who he manipulates, ultimately drawing himself away from God and blinding the manipulated soul from the light.

Control

Being a parent gives you neither the right of ownership or control of another soul, and yet man seeks to parent not only his own child with a view to ownership and control, but everyone within his reach in order to gain and maintain power. The need to control comes from fear. Seek God instead of control and know that you are powerless over all others. The affairs of others are for them and God to resolve. Not you.

Jealousy & Envy

You are blessed with more abundance than you could ever know. To seek ownership of what another has or to be jealous or envious of another's fortunes in any way deprives you of this knowledge. Learn to trust in God; to know that all you need, you have, even when you do not like it. Be assured that what you have is exactly what you need. Learn to live with God and you will experience the physical manifestation of God's love for you in abundance beyond your dreams.

Resentment

Resentment is created from unspoken anger, accumulated fear and selfish considerations. Learn to forgive others immediately for their transgressions and be not afraid to seek forgiveness from God and those who you have hurt on your journey past and present. In asking forgiveness you will empty your heart of the poison that destroys the soul, and peace freedom and love will be granted to you.

Gossip

What value gossip? Other than to the shell of the departed soul, that knows no joy. To enter the world of gossip is to join the ranks of the accusers, attackers and damned. Be honest in all your communications. Refuse gossip as you would the viper that would take your life for the moment of laxity when vigilance is overcome by the inquisitiveness for knowledge of falsehoods, that may cause the destruction of a naked spirit.

Bitterness & hatred

Sealed inside the heart and mind of its unwise jailer, bitterness and hatred is the creeping sickness that pervades the physical body perverting the cells of human life from the path of good health. Like the densest fog it clouds his vision from the cause of his physical disease. It has no value and only invades its master. Let go of these emotional parasites that will claim your life experience before you can.

Avoidance & Sloth

We know, see, hear and feel all things. Your experience is your opportunity, the opportunity that you have sought. It is our joy to grant you this journey and to give you eternal support to transcend that which you have come to learn. We seek no forgiveness for ensuring you the best chance of achieving your goal. Avoidance and sloth will only increase the difficulty of the lesson. Take courage and face that barrier which you have chosen to overcome and know that we stand beside the willing. With the knowledge and acceptance of this the spirit soars, the mind quickens, the body energises and the barrier disappears. The lesson is learned ,and the master appears from the sunken carcass.

Lies and Deceit

Distorting the beauty of what is given to you at rebirth only increases the weight of the cross you bear. Your path becomes distorted, long and dark. The lies and deceit are creating clouds that shroud the beauty of the soul within, attempting to extinguish the light of Christ that burns eternally inside you, extending the distance from that which you crave the most. Love! The light will never leave you. Live freely in the knowledge that you are perfect in your imperfection and that God created you without the need to lie and deceive. Allow yourself to be magnificent by living with God in honesty and know the freedom that truth restores.

Fear

The ultimate challenge; the prize beyond all prizes. To be free of fear is to know that God exists. That you are in God's world. That you are in God's protection. That all that is, is because God deems it so. That everything in God's world is perfection. That freedom from fear is merely a choice away. That freedom from dis-ease is yours for the asking.

It is fear that is the root of all evils that drives man to all his pain, to dysfunction and dis-ease. Fear knows no mercy and waits for the unsuspecting soul to wander past its lair, for it absorbs you into its control. It knows those who have no defences against its power and wields its victory over you in the creation of destruction within you like a razor edged sabre slicing through your heart.

Wherever you are, call and we will be there. Whoever you are, ask and you will be given. Whatever your pain know that in seeking us it is diminished. Fear cannot and will not breach the unbreakable Might of Our Love for all of you. It is in God's love that you will find your peaceful sanctuary.

Humility

Remain humble in all your affairs. True greatness is found in the silence of the humble soul who seeks not to become fulfilled through self acclaimed honour, but is glorified through unselfish acts of kindness.

Honesty

Your life becomes filled with reason to be dishonest, for the pressures to deceive created by man are hard to withstand. Know, all of you, that to follow the path of honesty will deliver you into freedom, a freedom that will embrace your soul with love, the freedom that you all seek, and a freedom that only truth can deliver. To lie is to shackle yourself into darkness and pain. Leave it behind you now no matter how big or small you perceive the lie to be. The honest who remain unbending, will know a new peace, a peace that is only found in the kingdom of honesty.

Living with God

Kindness

It is easier to be kind than it is not to be. Yet so many choose the path of hurt, for this is what you have learned from each other. Learn then that as you sow, then so shall you reap. Change your actions and learn the pleasure of giving a kindness in the simple form of a smile, a warm hand, a kind word. Allow the spirit within you to connect with the spirit in another and see how you can free that soul from the confines of their own prison, the prison that is isolation and solitude created from fear. Open your heart and your eyes to the needs of others. Choose each day to commit a random act of kindness for an unsuspecting neighbour, without seeking reward for your act, or even allowing them knowledge of who the benefactor of this kindness is and then you shall reap the rewards of a loving God.

Trust

Through fear and your experience you have learned to mistrust all others, which now threatens to rob you of the ultimate joy of life, as the mistrust now stands between you and the fruit of your journey as gifted by God.

This gift from God is to experience unconditional love while in physical form.

Shutting down and mistrusting will lead you away from God, for as you close down to pain then so shall you close yourself to love. Each and everyone of you has been granted this gift; it is only fear of being hurt that denies you the taste of loves flavour.

Have faith that in remaining open and trusting others you remain open to receiving, even though you may *be hurt in the process. Keep trusting. You will not be disappointed.*

Do not commit the crime of denying yourself this honour through lack of trust. Have faith in God's word to you, that unconditional love is yours for the taking, when you have the courage to face your fear of trusting.

First learn to be trustworthy. Give no man reason to mistrust you.

Patience & Tolerance

With self, for yours is a life journey, not a sprint, but a continuous learning that is an upward spiral of spiritual growth towards enlightenment, towards the mastery of self. Allow your life mistakes and crosses to become opportunities rather than a heavier burden.

Demonstrate patience and tolerance with those who are behind you, and teach, through the demonstration of your being, the wisdom of God that is within you.

Dignity & Integrity

You are made in the image of God. Do not fear it. You are no greater or lesser than any other man, and no other shall steal from you what you do not allow them to. Maintain dignity and integrity in all areas of your life, and by doing so you honour who and what you are. The naked pauper, who upholds the glory of himself by retaining what no earthly being can strip from him, is richer than the richest king, who has sold his dignity and integrity to hold on to his crown.

Love

All of you, who have lost your way by seeking the love of another to find fulfilment, come to me and find yourself again. Only through first loving yourself can you learn to love another. To seek from someone else that which *you are unable to give to your own being, will suck the life blood from their souls and cause the ultimate destruction of all relationships. In loving yourself you love God. By loving God you are filled with an inexhaustible abundance of unconditional love, which will free the spirit of the chosen being that decides to walk beside you into heaven and know everlasting love.*

It is man that has driven away from his being, his own ability to feel love for himself by not understanding that self love does not mean selfish, self seeking or selfishness. Man scorns the thought of self love through fear or the opposite and allows himself to succumb to extremes of vanity and inflated ego, each one being as ugly as the other. The dis-ease that all mankind suffers is the void that is created by fear!

Fear creates self hatred, lack of self worth, poor self-esteem and is the beginning of all forms of physical, mental, emotional and spiritual disease. It is overcoming fear that will deliver you into love and free you from this illness. It is the decision and action of choosing to live with God that will deliver you from fear of all things.

Choose to live these lessons. Create new actions in your life with them and you will choose to live with God. Then you will enter paradise and truly know Peace, Freedom and Love here on Earth.

Teachings from Sananda

I am sure that many will look at this and say
   "hang on a minute this guy is just copying what everyone else has already done and is just regurgitating what has been said a thousand times over."

I thought you just said at the beginning of this book that you accepted you had no power over what was written herein?

I did, but they will ask.

Something to understand is that we have been giving the same message since God made man and the world began. It never changes, we choose to deliver it in many different ways so that more people have the opportunity of getting the message and we will continue to choose whatever medium we need to do so. We have not given any single person or group specific ownership of communicating God's word.

Raven

I see.

So through the writing of this book we are offering yet another channel of communication that continues to give our guidance and help to those that seek it. We have just decided to choose you on this occasion.

Does this answer one of my all time questions, then, of how God speaks to me, because of all the times that I have sat and asked and thought that no one was listening or could be bothered to answer?

Yes, it does, Raven. There is never a time when an answer is not given to those who ask. It is just that the questioner often misses the answer, because he/she is expecting it to come in a specific way. For instance, we speak through all types of different mediums ranging from books to songs to animals. The different ways for us to communicate is endless and importantly so. Not all men read books or listen to songs or take note of the messages that animals give, so we have to choose such a diverse range of channels.

Are you saying, then, that I am a channel for God's communication?

Living with God

We are, as is every human being, plant and creature to name the simple forms of communication on the planet Earth. Have you ever noticed the amount of songs that have been written about love. It is the most written about subject and people like Elton John, Madonna, The Beatles, Michael Jackson, Phil Collins, to name a few, are all channels we use for communication. They are all inspired with songs of love. Love is what man craves more than anything, and loving self and one another is the greatest message that we wish to communicate.

Are they aware of this?

Ask them! It may awaken some of them to themselves and what they are doing, for not all channels realise that they are communicating God's word and may not wish to accept it for fear of the word "GOD". For others it may come as a revelation.

I don't know these people, and I thought that in order to be a channel we all had to sit cross legged on the floor all day saying Ohm or looking starry eyed and not of this planet, special, new age traveller types.

Everyone is special, Raven, no one is greater or lesser than the next man. All are equal. Many people get lost in spiritualism and often hide behind it, so that they don't have to look at themselves any more. Often ego becomes the driving force behind such people that call themselves spiritual, and they start to believe themselves to be better than others. People love to consider that communicating with God needs some special kind of talent and that those who do so are mystics or cranks, depending on the point of view of the one judging. You know what we feel about those who judge. Man is all too quick to point out the shortcomings of someone else in order to avoid sight of his own character defects. Everyone is a channel for God.

The other day I received an e-mail from a group I used to be involved with inviting me to a channelling to receive what? And it stops there, because some of the words that were being used in this message to me, I don't understand, or they use a different language like Indian, and so many times when I have attended something spiritual I have just left confused saying what the hell was all that about. They talk about planets aligning and things that just confuse me.

Living with God

God is not confusing Raven. Nor is the message we give. We choose to communicate in whatever way is necessary to get the message across. Remember that many people who are looking for God find the path through all kinds of ways. For some need to focus on another human who to them has special talents and can lead them to God. If that is the only way for these people to find God, then so be it. You are angry with these teachers and leaders for confusing you, or is it that you consider them to be masquerading as channels. As I have told you many times, what value does anger have in this case? None. Are you not judging these people yourself? Would it not be better to be an example rather than a judge? If ever you are confused by the message of God then ask the teacher to explain. All good teachers love to explain to those who ask.

So why do I feel angry about these people who call themselves spiritual? I have seen them being all misty eyed and loving, spouting words of peace and love and the next minute abusing each other and doing exactly what they preach not to do.

It is simple. Because you are judging them. Stop judging them and become an example instead. Even teachers are not immune to learning and growing. It is only when they consider themselves beyond learning and growing that they have then become subjected to their own ego. Rather than being angry or judgemental yourself, demonstrate through your own example of being the word of God.

Remember. You and all humans, first and foremost, are spiritual beings having a physical experience.

What does that mean?

It means that you are a spiritual being Raven. You and all living creatures are part of the collective consciousness,

Whoa!! What's that?.

It means that the essence that is you beyond your physical body is as I am. You are part of us and we are part of you. Every person you see is connected in the same way. We all come from the same soup so to speak. The energy that makes up the spirit that is you, makes up the spirit that is everyone else including us, hence the statements we and us rather than me and I. God is not an individual. God is everyone and everything as are you. That takes care of the word "spiritual". Now for the word "being" and take this in, "human BEING" Got it?

No!

Raven, the word "being" that is used in the spiritual sense and the human sense is the same word. What does it mean? It means BEING. Through BEING you become the message of God. That is, we ask you and all mankind to BE rather than judge, condemn, manipulate, deceive, and gossip and so on. Live a life of being God. Simple enough?

Raven

I think so! Rather then me trying to teach someone what they are doing wrong better, I demonstrate the right way through my being.

At last we think you have got it.

Except the part that says being God?

Explain?

You said "Live a life of being God".

Yes, we did. We mean being God. As we just said, we are all part of the same consciousness. The energy that makes up you and all others in the universe including us is the same. Therefore, you are God and we are you. The trick here, that is if you want to call it a trick, is to bring the spiritual connection that we all have into the physical through your being. Hence Living with God.

Are you saying that I am God and so is everyone else.

In simple terms, yes.

Does this mean that I have got to act like God?

No. Acting is not being. Being as God is, and demonstrating it in your life, will give others the opportunity to see that if one human can do it, then so can they. Some time ago we gave guidance which ended up as a book. This was channelled by us through two mediums called Bill and Bob. This book was the guidelines for living for mankind, who would do well to study it take the principles that you learn from it and then implement them into your life.

What is the book called?

Alcoholics Anonymous. Fondly known by those who use it as The Big Book.

Are you suggesting that we are all alcoholics?

No, I am saying that at a time when man had no answer to the Dis-ease you call alcoholism, these two men called forth help from God, and we answered in the form of The Big Book. Since its creation countless thousands of men and women have been freed from countless forms of dis-eases that have baffled man not only alcoholism.

Raven

There is not a human being walking the planet that is free from dis-ease of one form or another. Man has chosen to try and put these dis-eases right through man made chemicals and other means that have entirely missed the core issue of all dis-ease.

You and all others are spiritual beings having a physical experience, and it is only when man wakes up to the need to heal the spirit, that an end to such human maladies can start to change.

How do you heal the spirit?

All of mankind comes from the same place which is Love. The goal is to experience love while in a physical form. So often man has tried to practice love as they have become aware of this fact yet still not achieved the ultimate goal, because the focus has been on loving others. We hear man say, I am loving, caring and considerate. Many are except for the kind of love that is still missing. love and acceptance of self.

When you fell in love, as I know you have, your whole being was immersed in the experience of love. Your entire focus was on the person you fell in love with. You felt totally immersed in the feelings of love with that person, as if the rest of the world did not exist. Your entire world was now wrapped up in that other person. You were happier than you had ever been in your life. Bills, debts, life in the form of fear no longer existed until the realisation came of the potential loss of that person. Then all hell broke loose. This fear starts to create a pain inside you, so then you start to create all types of controls within your relationship to avoid this loss all of which is the beginning of the end of the love. All of this happens because of the lack of love and acceptance of self. we will talk more of healing the spirit in our next book. shall we?

I would like that.

For now, Raven let us just enjoy what we have learned and practice the guidelines we have given you until they become natural actions in your daily life.

Thank you for everything!

We are forever here to serve you.

About the Author

As a young boy and into my adult years all I ever sought was success, in all areas of my life, the same as probably every other human being on the planet. The problem was, without the right guidelines on how to live my life and achieve this elusive success, I ended up venturing down paths that could only lead me to disaster, a place that I became all too familiar with.

Knowing the words to a song does not mean that you can sing it:

I chose role models in life that I thought, were upstanding pillars of society, unfortunately, just because I created an image of myself based on how they looked and behaved, did not mean that I was like them. I missed the vital ingredients, the parts that are not seen, the bits that guide us to establishing who and what we are, what our purpose for being here is, what we like and dislike, how we act and react to situations. These parts were not available to me. It meant that I became a social chameleon, unable to live in a world that I did not understand. A guaranteed recipe for sickness, disaster and destruction.

After forty six years of pain, loss, emptiness and failure, I looked to the only place that I had never dared to consider was real. I found what I was looking for, a teacher beyond compare.

The evidence of what I now experience in my life is all I need to confirm the truth. I am privileged to be able to pass on to you the gift that our teacher has given me and offers to all that seek it in this book.

We wish you Peace, Love and Freedom in all your affairs

Raven

Printed in the United Kingdom
by Lightning Source UK Ltd.
127772UK00002B/19-36/P